I Heard You Can Draw
Wild Animals!
A step-by-step drawing guide

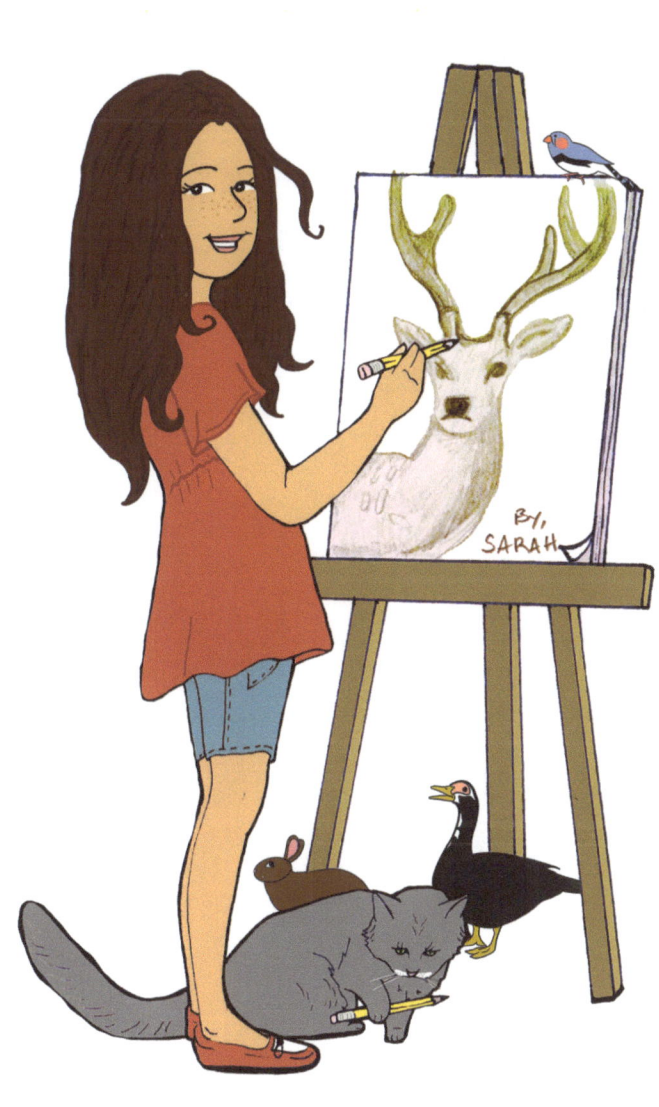

Art Class with Ms. S. Books

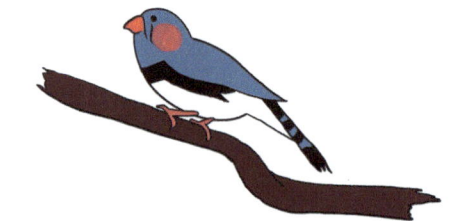

This book is for all of the kids
out there who love to draw!

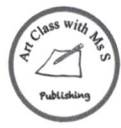

Art Class with Ms S

ISBN-10: 0-9896490-6-7
ISBN-13: 978-0-9896490-6-3

BISAC: Juvenile Nonfiction / Art / Drawing

I Heard You Can Draw

Wild Animals!

A step-by-step drawing guide

Art Class with Ms. S. Books

This book belongs to:

_____

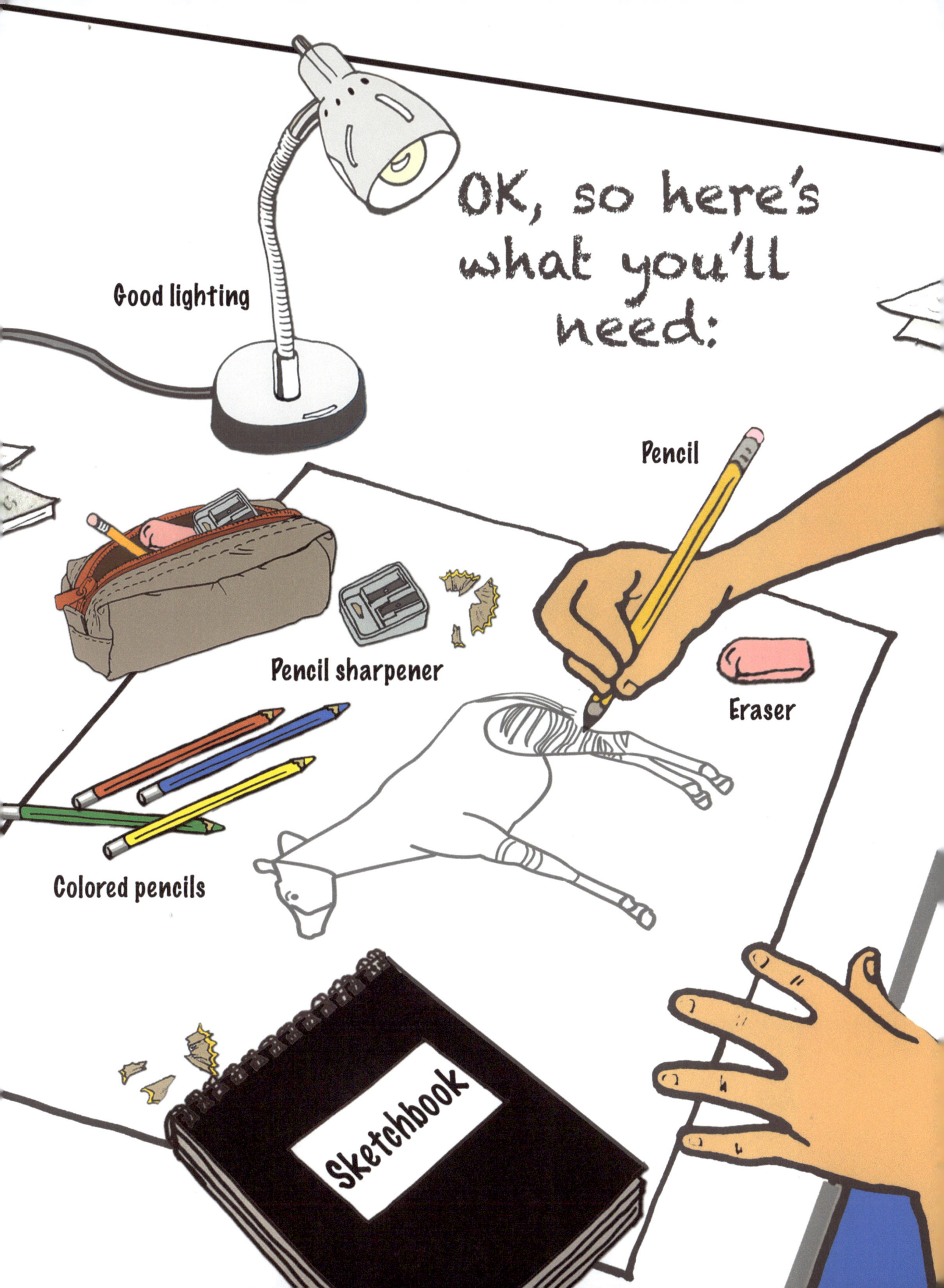

I Heard You Can Draw a...
Mandrill!

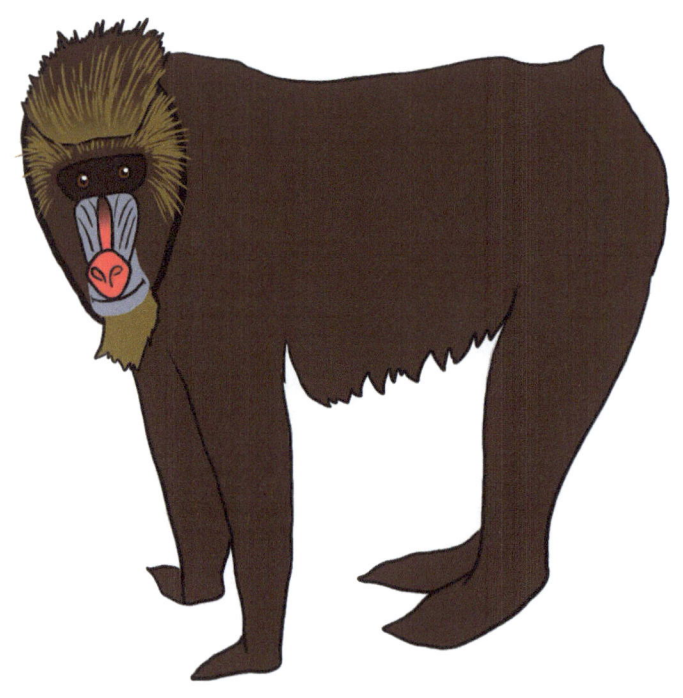

Mandrills are the largest monkeys. They live in West Africa.
Did you notice their colorful faces?

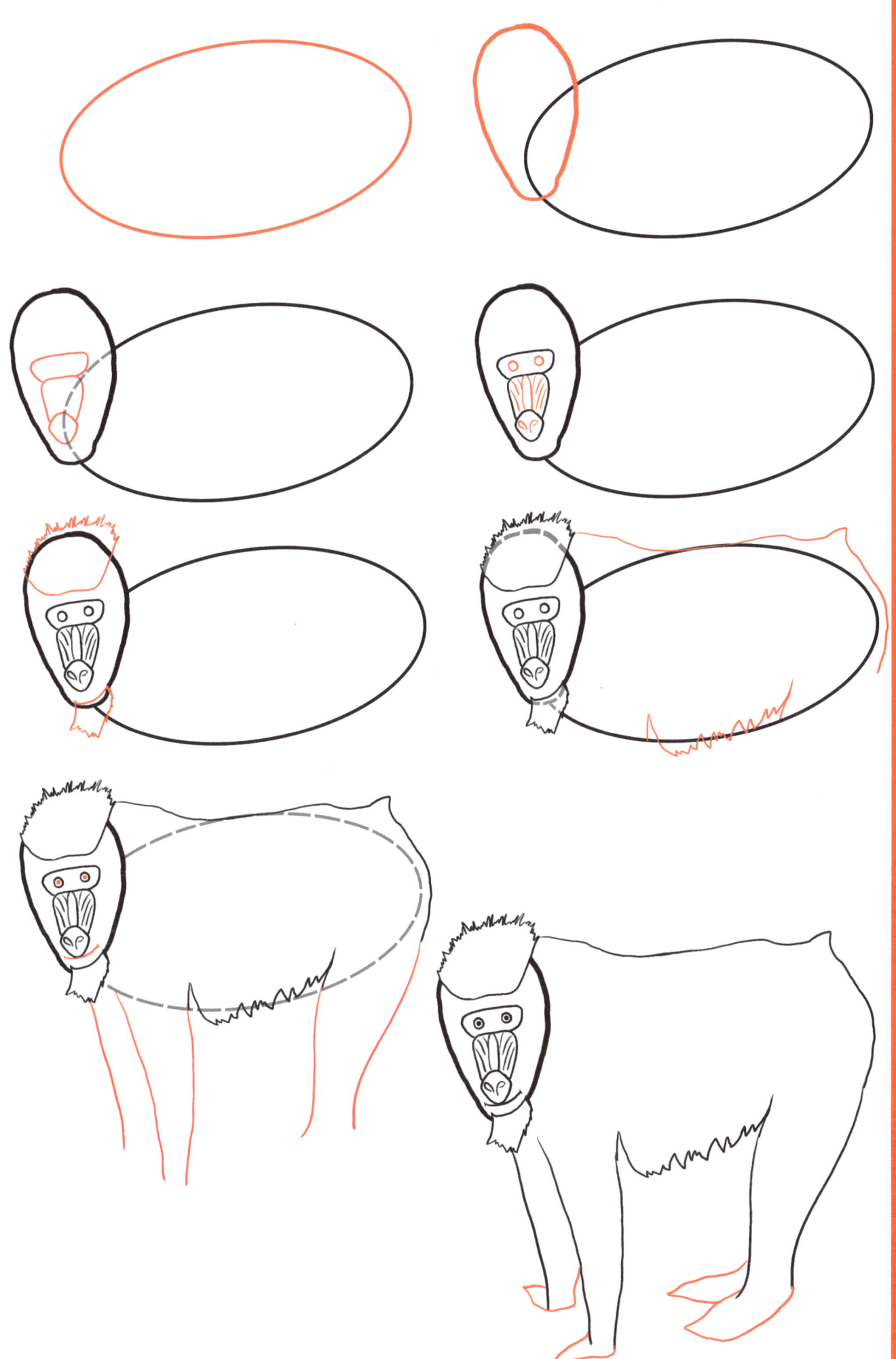

3

I Heard You Can Draw a...
Pheasant!

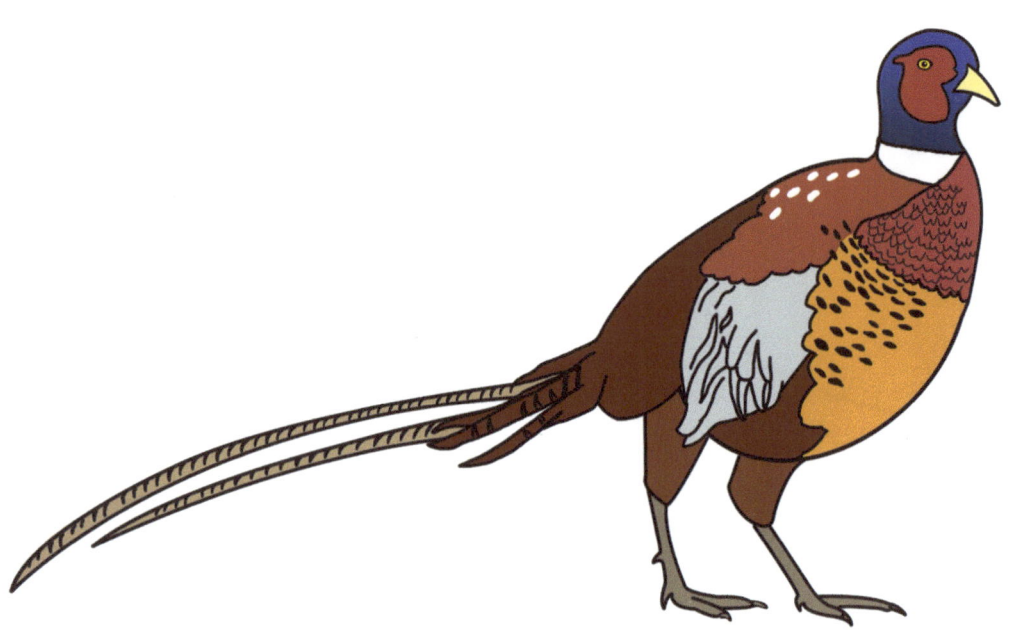

Ring-Necked Pheasants are native to Asia, although now they live in many parts of the world. Pheasants can fly if they have to, but you will mostly find them on the ground and not in the sky. Pheasants are one of the most hunted birds by man.

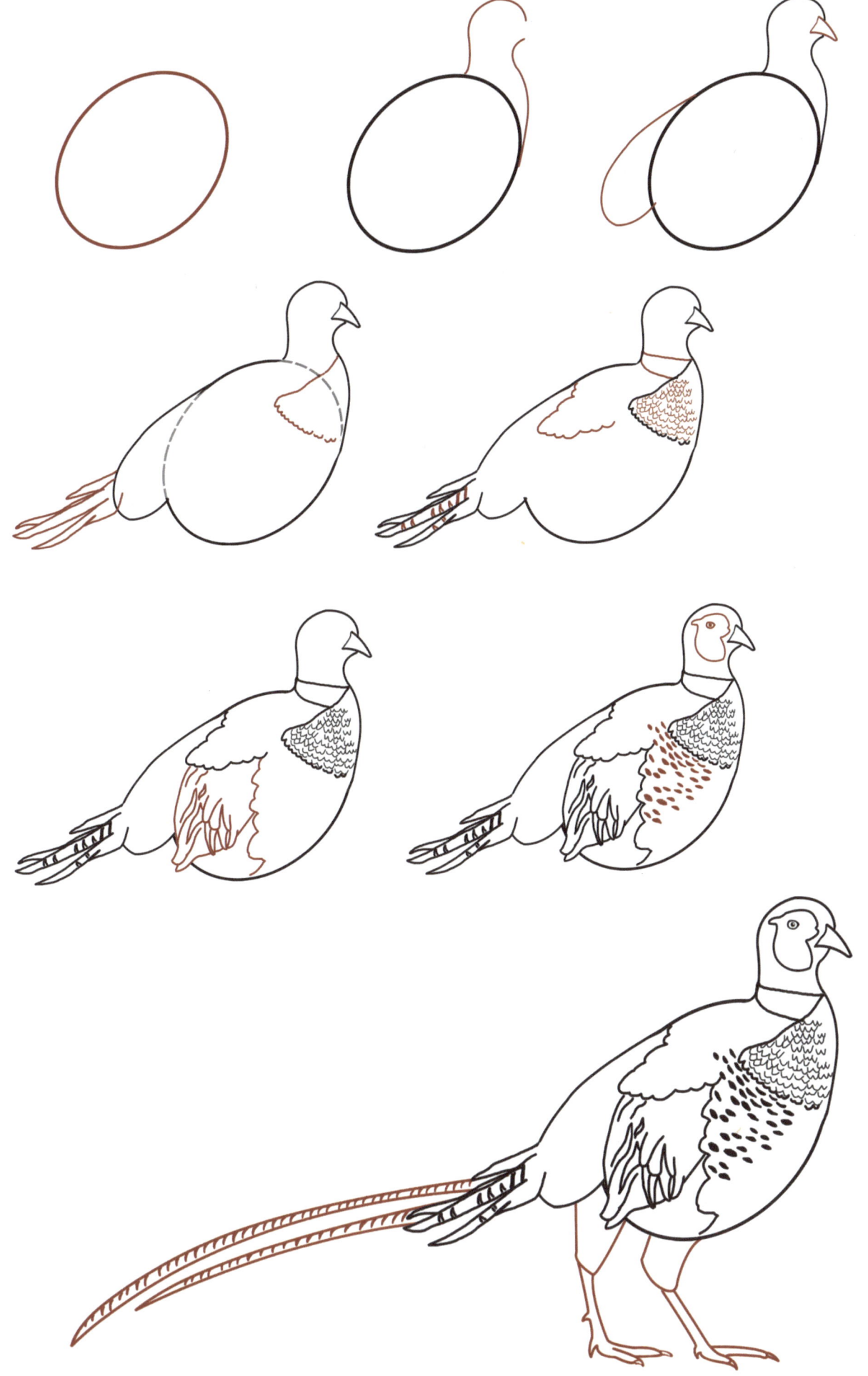

I Heard You Can Draw a...
Deer!

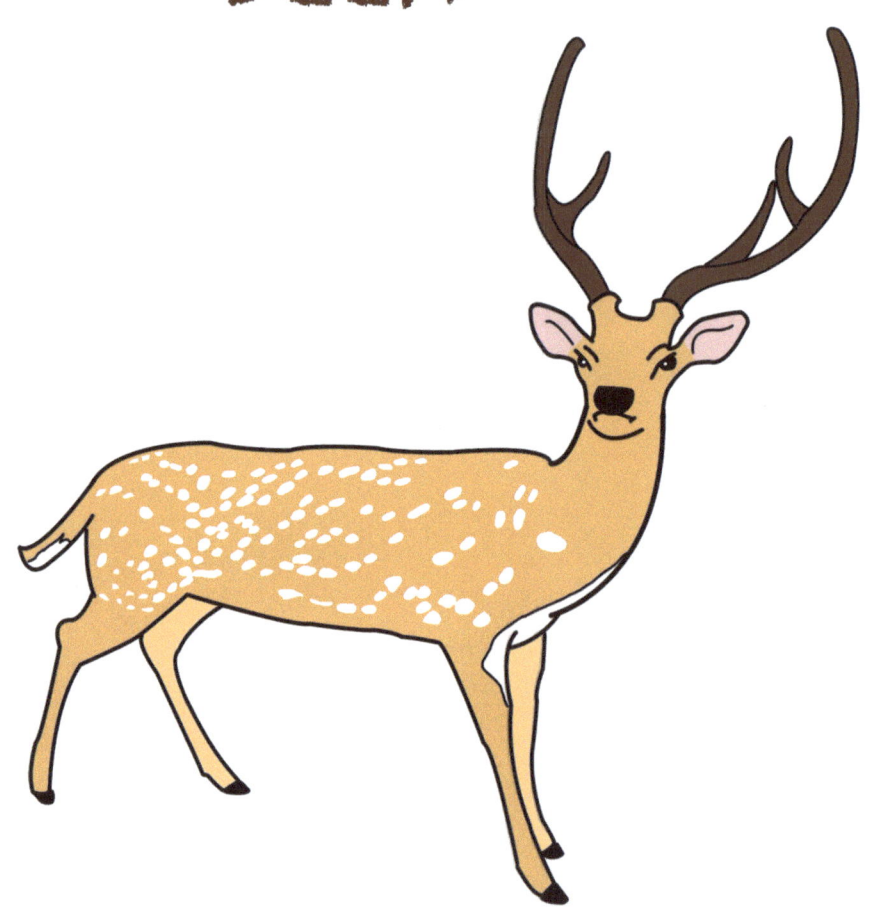

Deer live in the woodlands of North America through Central America.
An adult male deer is called a buck. Only male deer have antlers.
The female deer is called a doe, and their babies are called fawns.

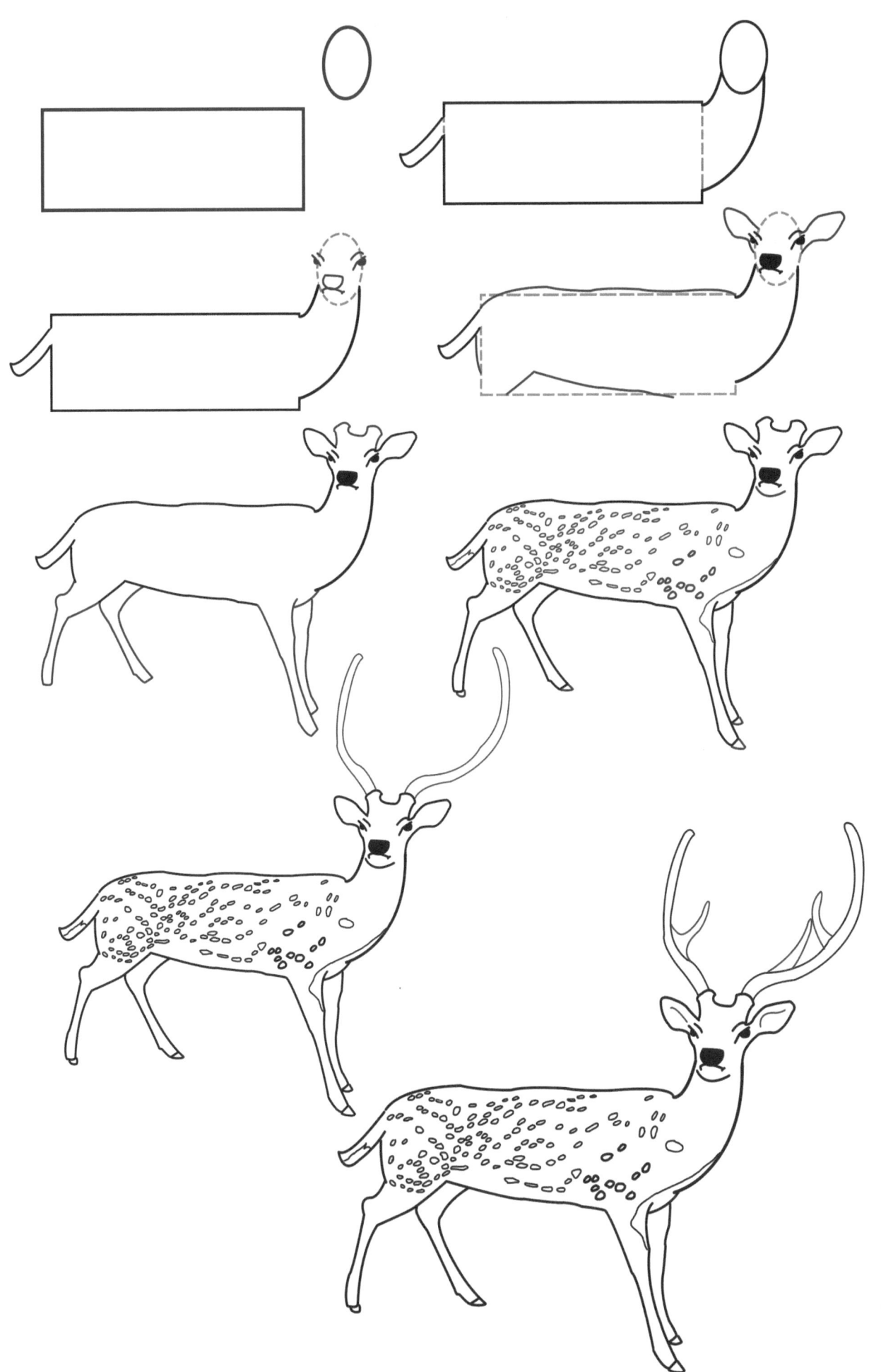

I Heard You Can Draw a...
Finch!

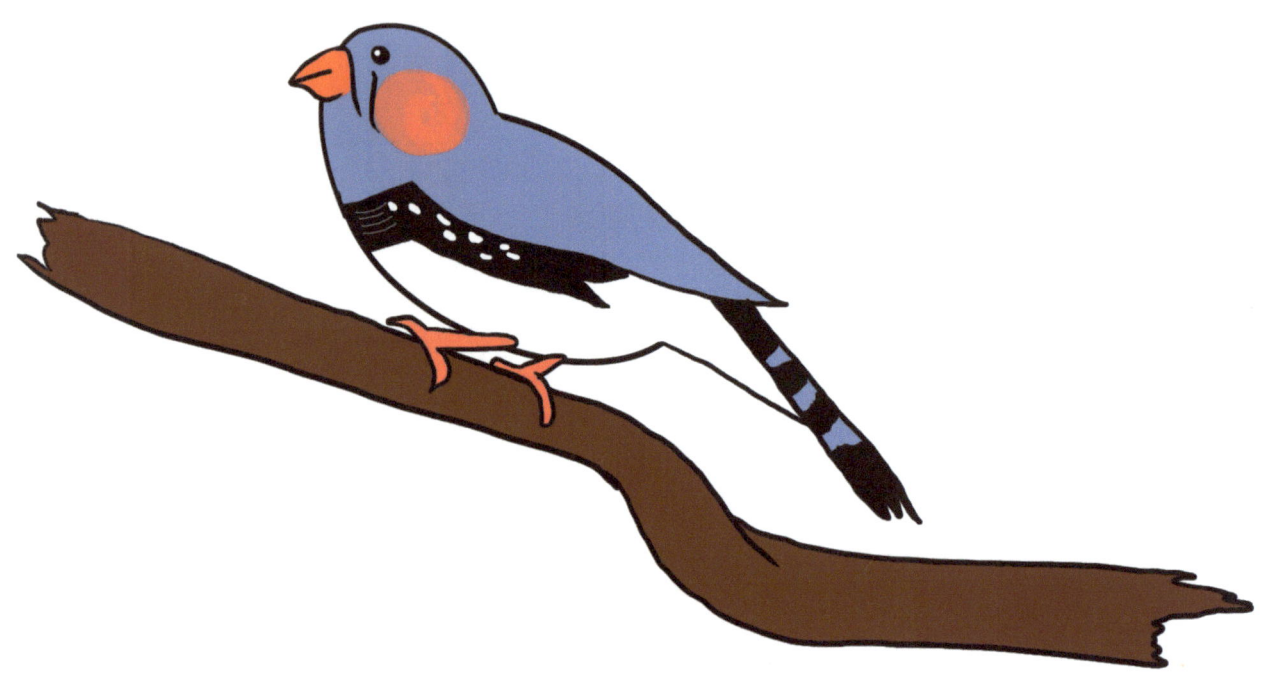

The Zebra Finch is a bird found in Australia.
They have bright orange beaks shaped like a triangle,
and they are very loud singers!

8

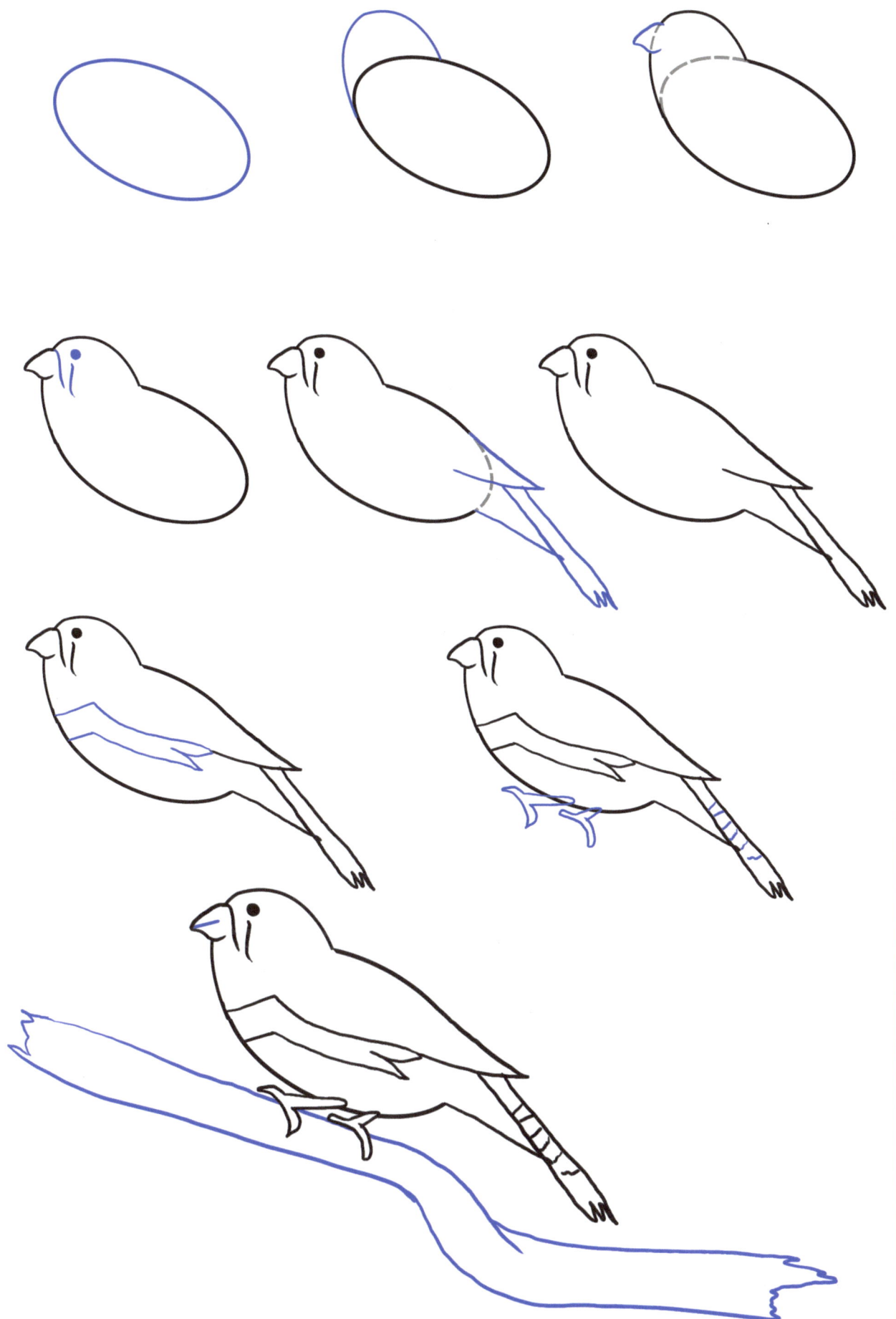

I Heard You Can Draw a...
Komodo Dragon!

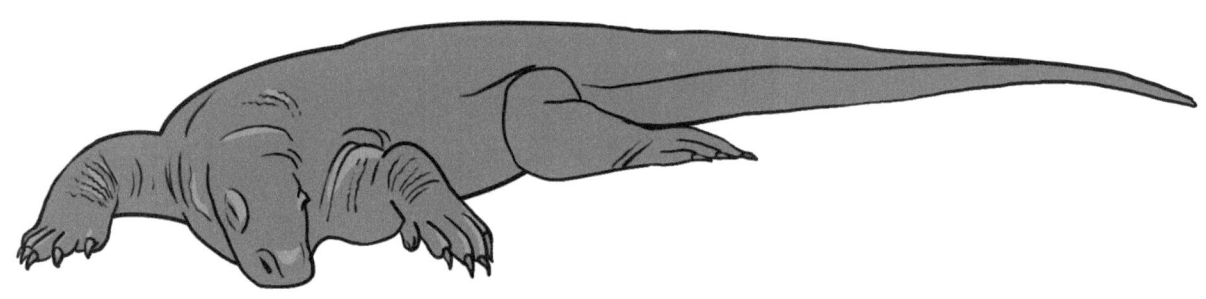

Komodo Dragons are the largest lizards. They can grow to be 10 feet long!
They can eat animals as large as deer, and they have very sharp teeth.
They live in Indonesia and are considered to be endangered.

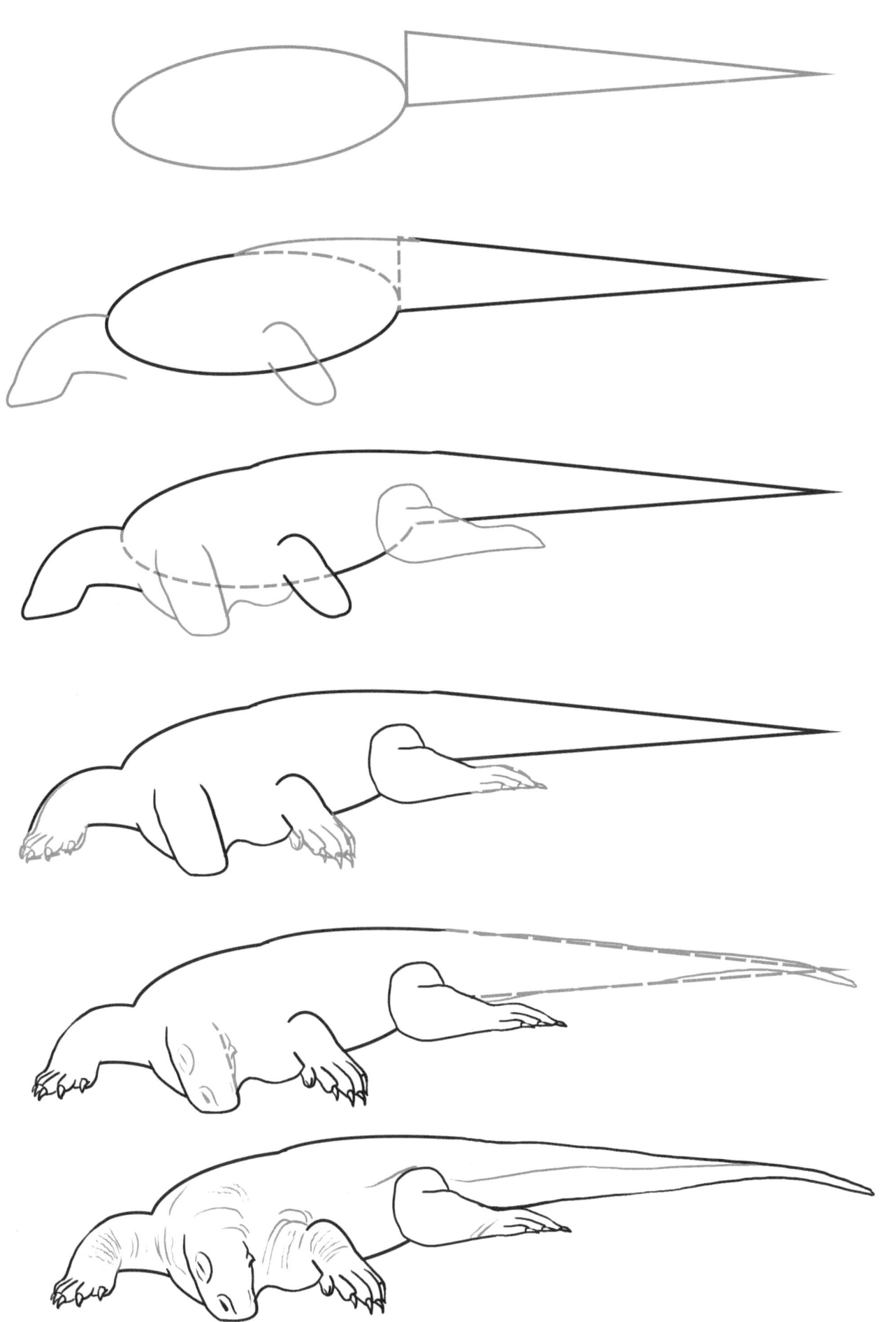

11

I Heard You Can Draw a...
Camel!

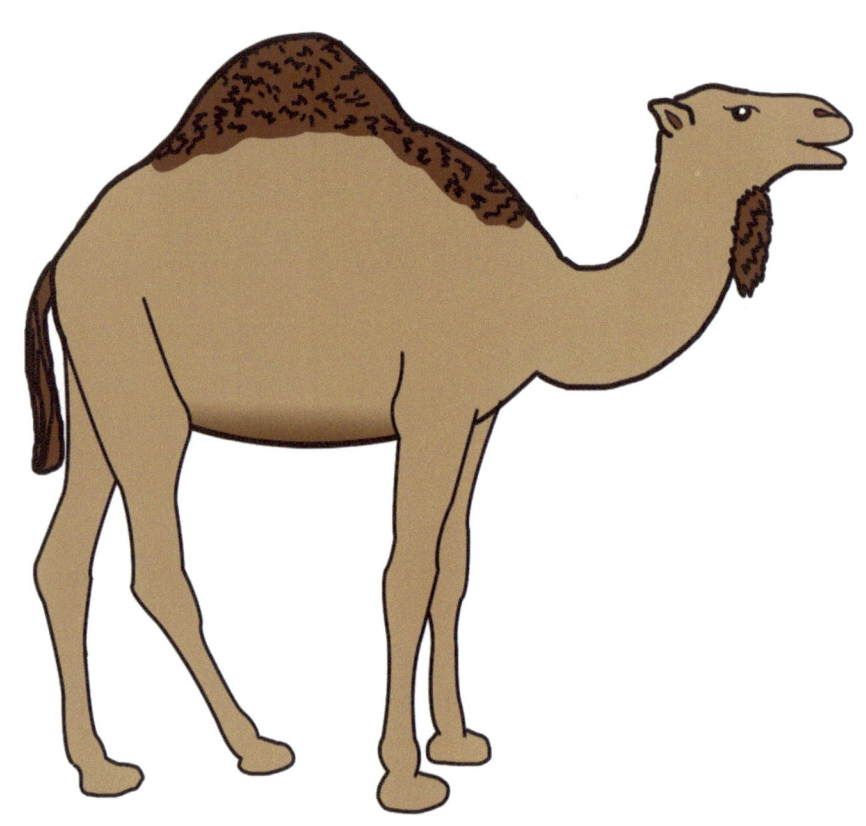

Dromedary camels have one hump, which is made of fat.
Dromedary camels live in Northern Africa and the Middle East.
They can survive in the desert without water for long periods of time!

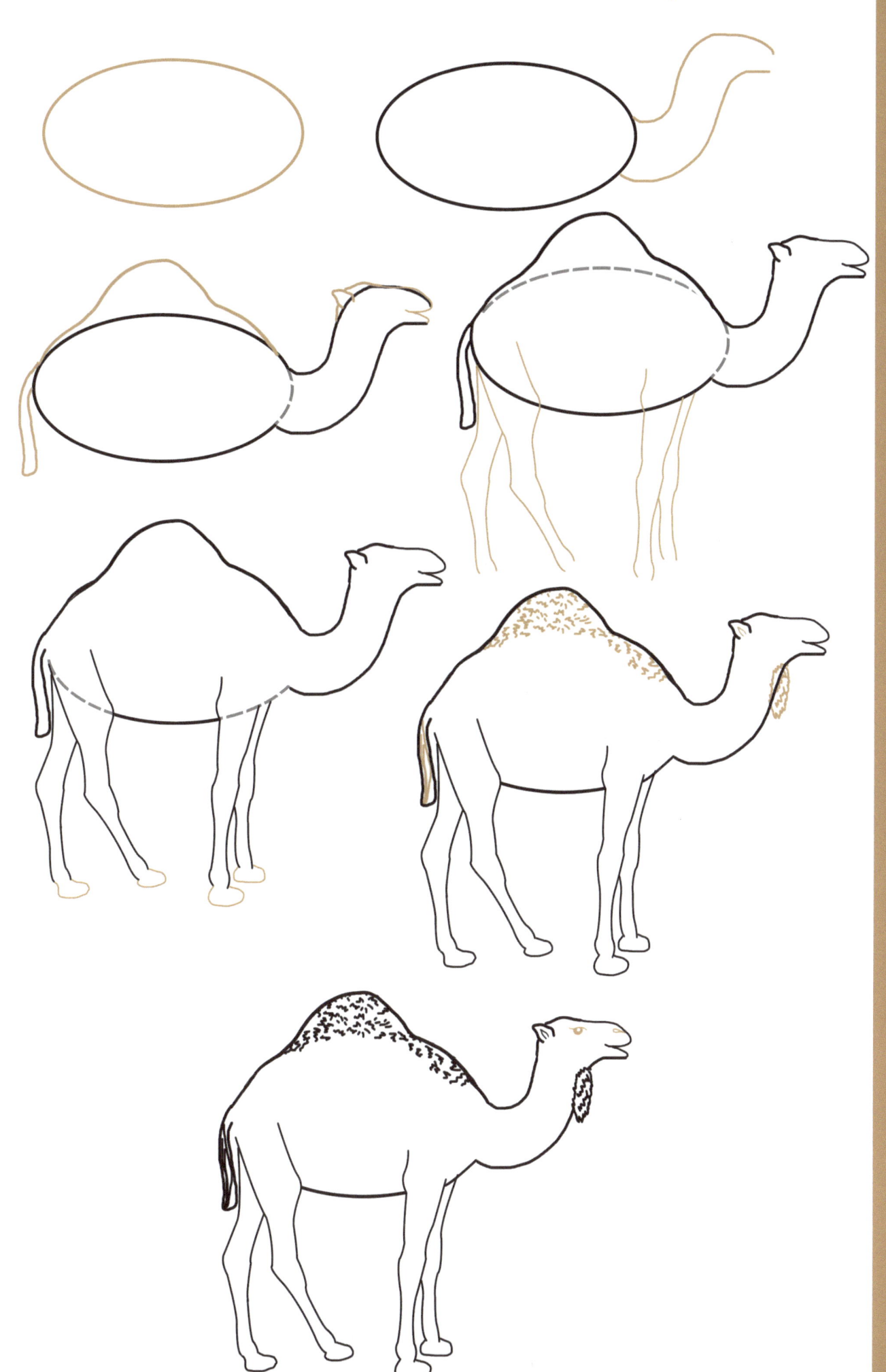

13

I Heard You Can Draw a...
Muscovy Duck!

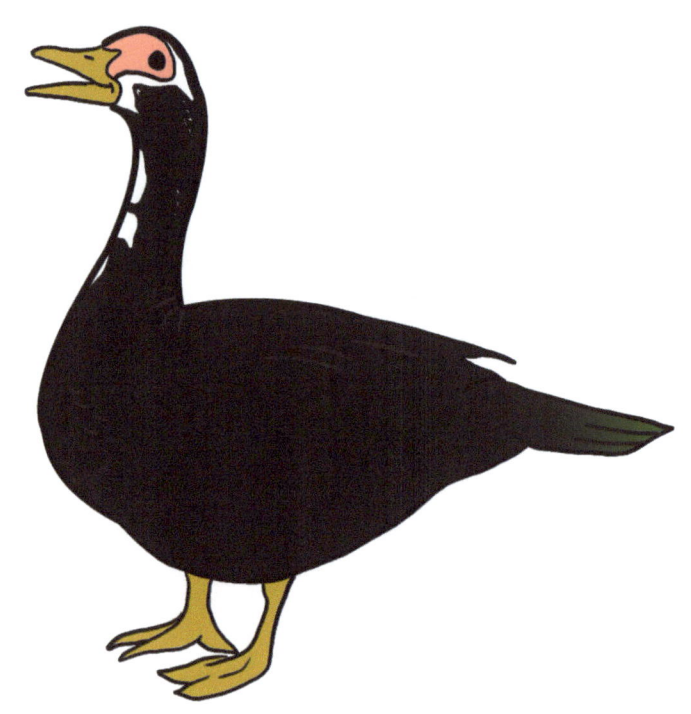

Muscovy ducks live in Central and South America and in some parts of the United States. They are dark black in color with white patches.

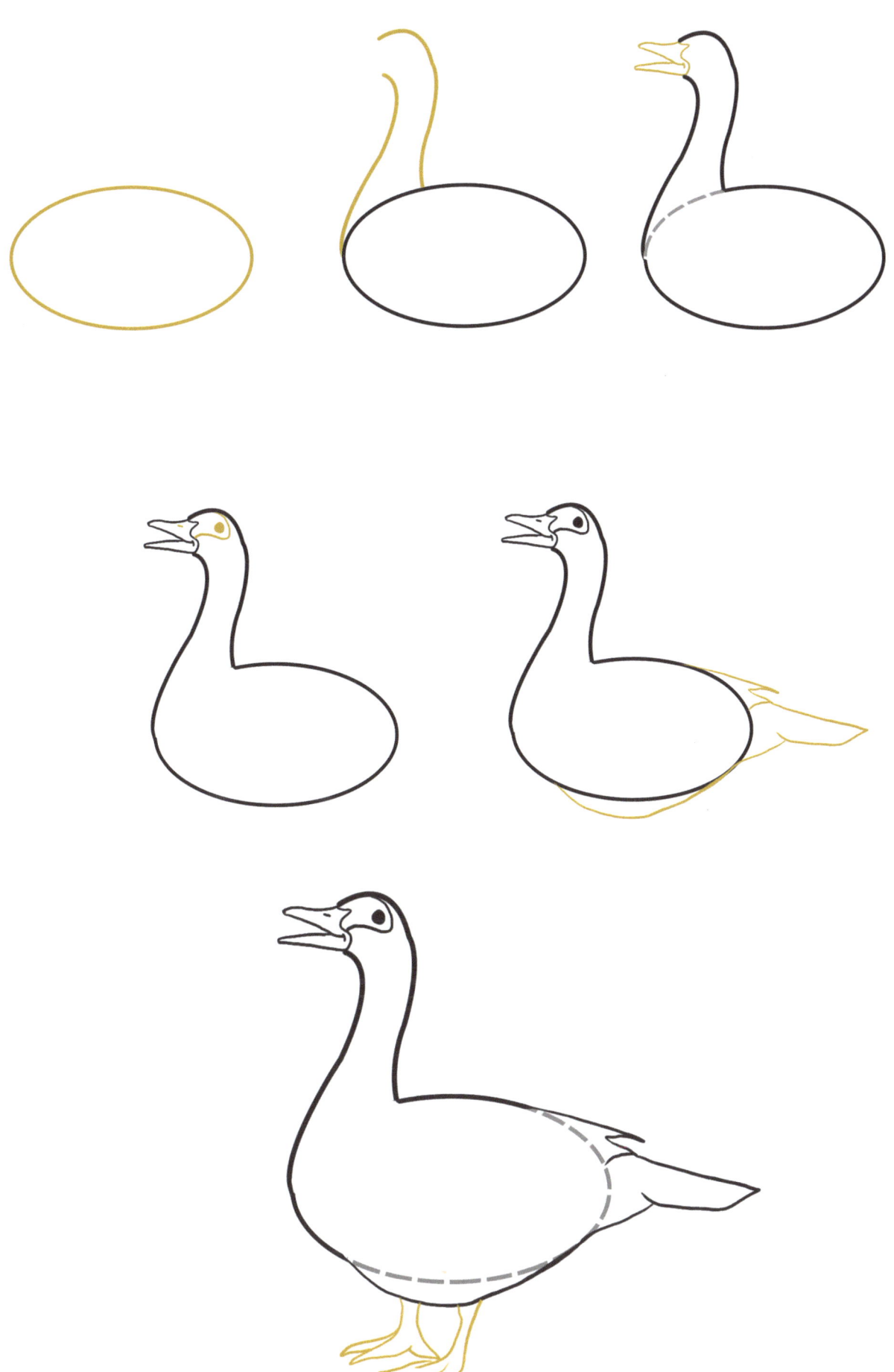

I Heard You Can Draw a...
Crane!

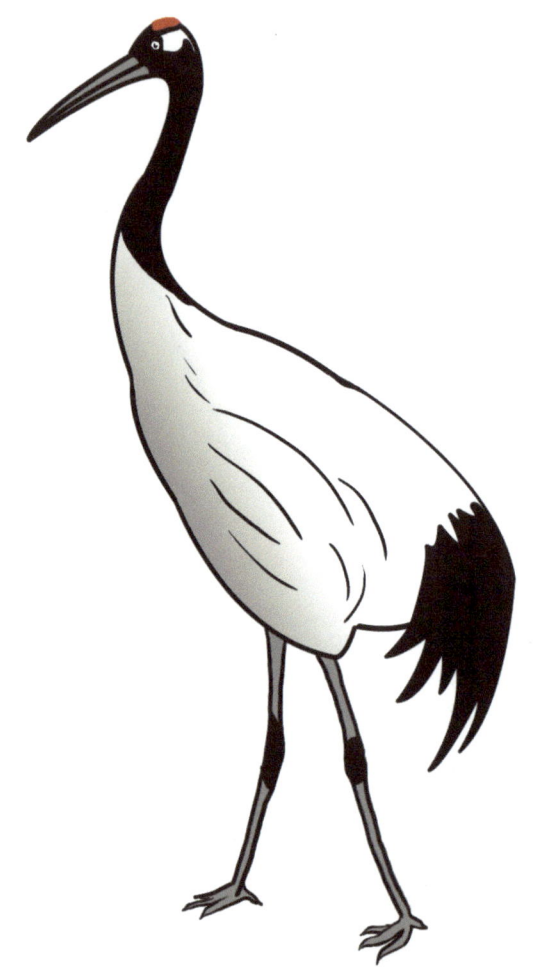

Red-crowned cranes live in East Asia. They love to dance
and they symbolize good luck and happiness!

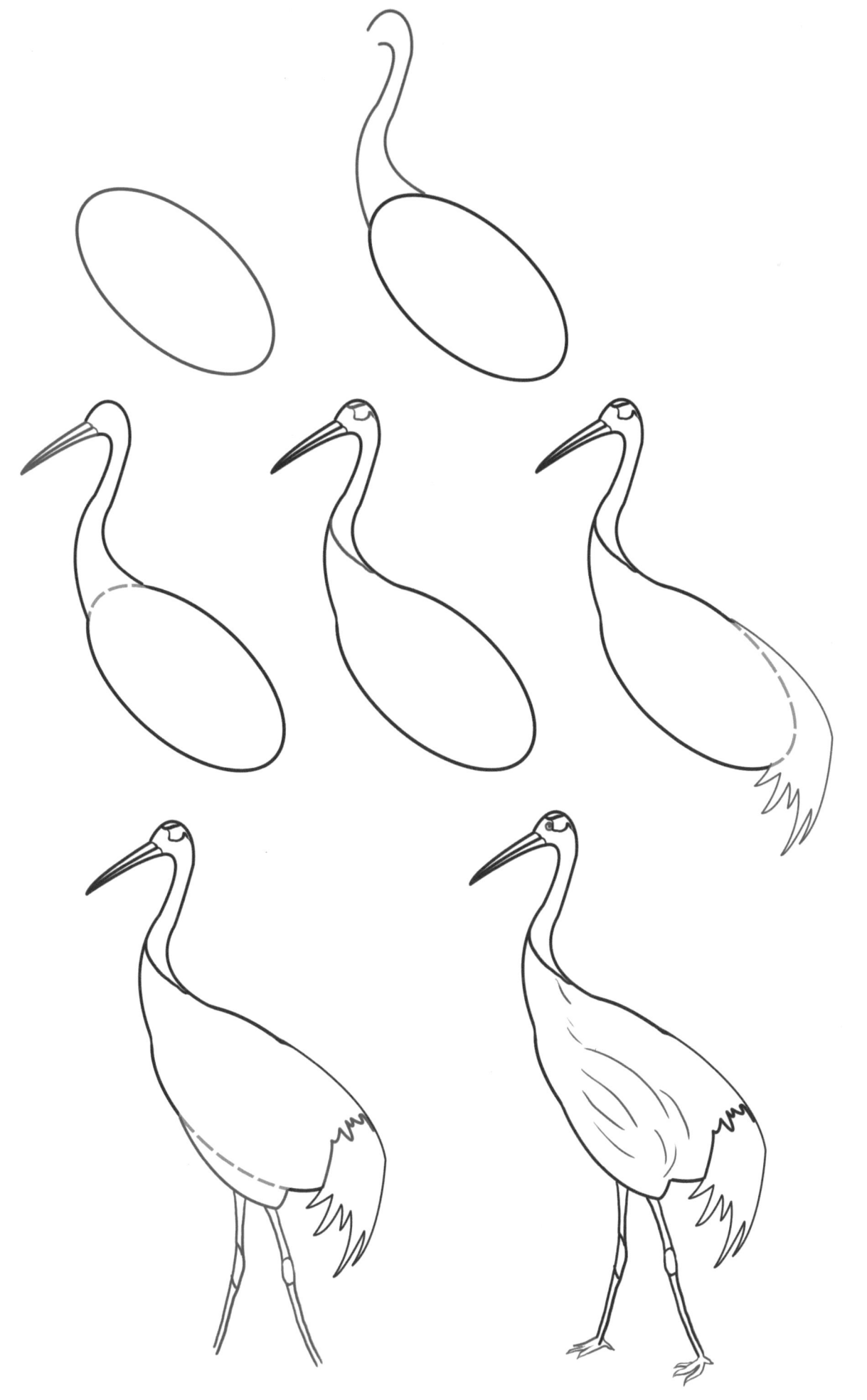

17

I Heard You Can Draw a...
Zebra!

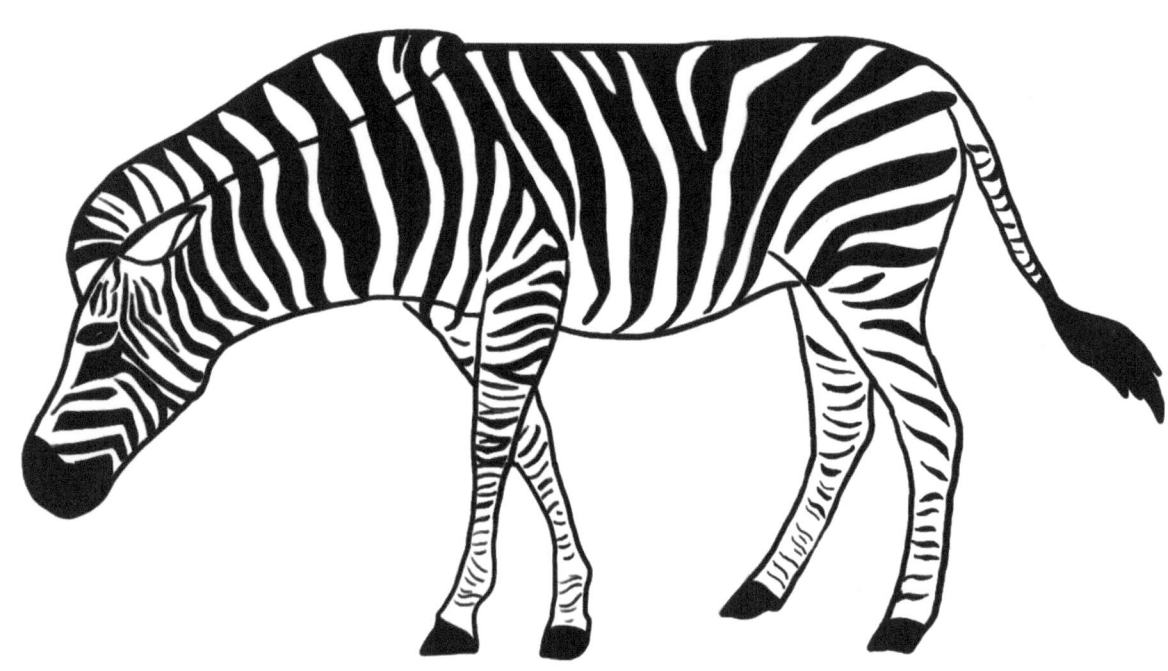

Zebras have beautiful black and white stripes and every zebra has a unique pattern! They live in Africa and they are part of the horse family.

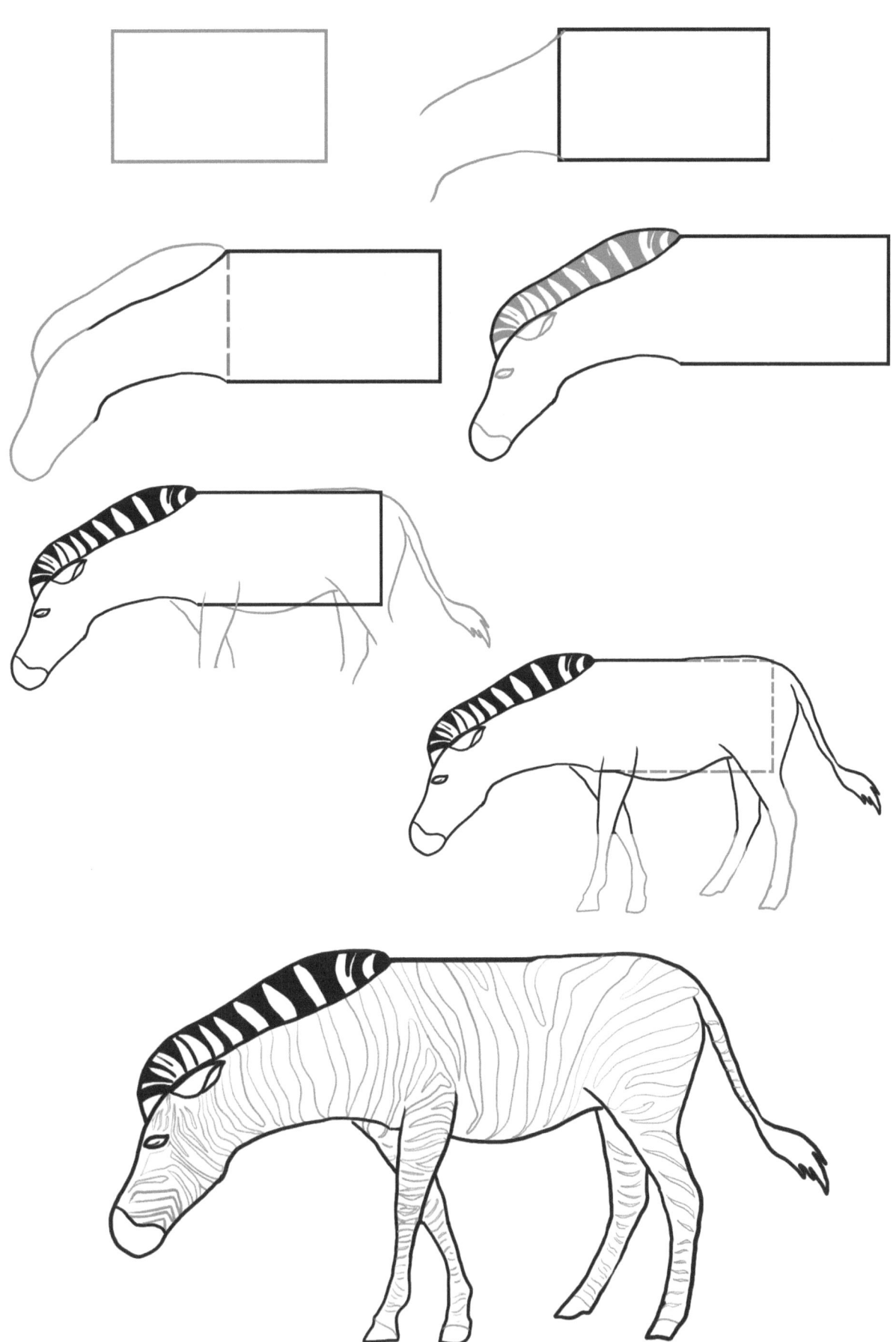

19

I Heard You Can Draw a...
Lion!

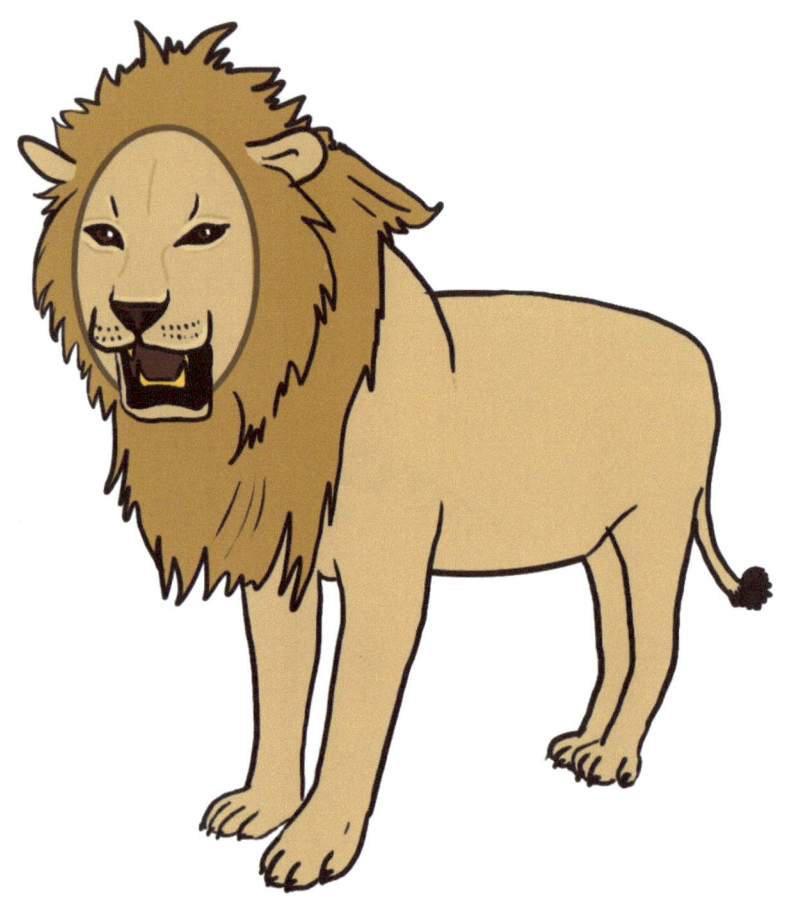

Lions live in Africa in groups called prides.
Male lions have a mane around their necks. They have
very loud roars which can be heard from 5 miles away!

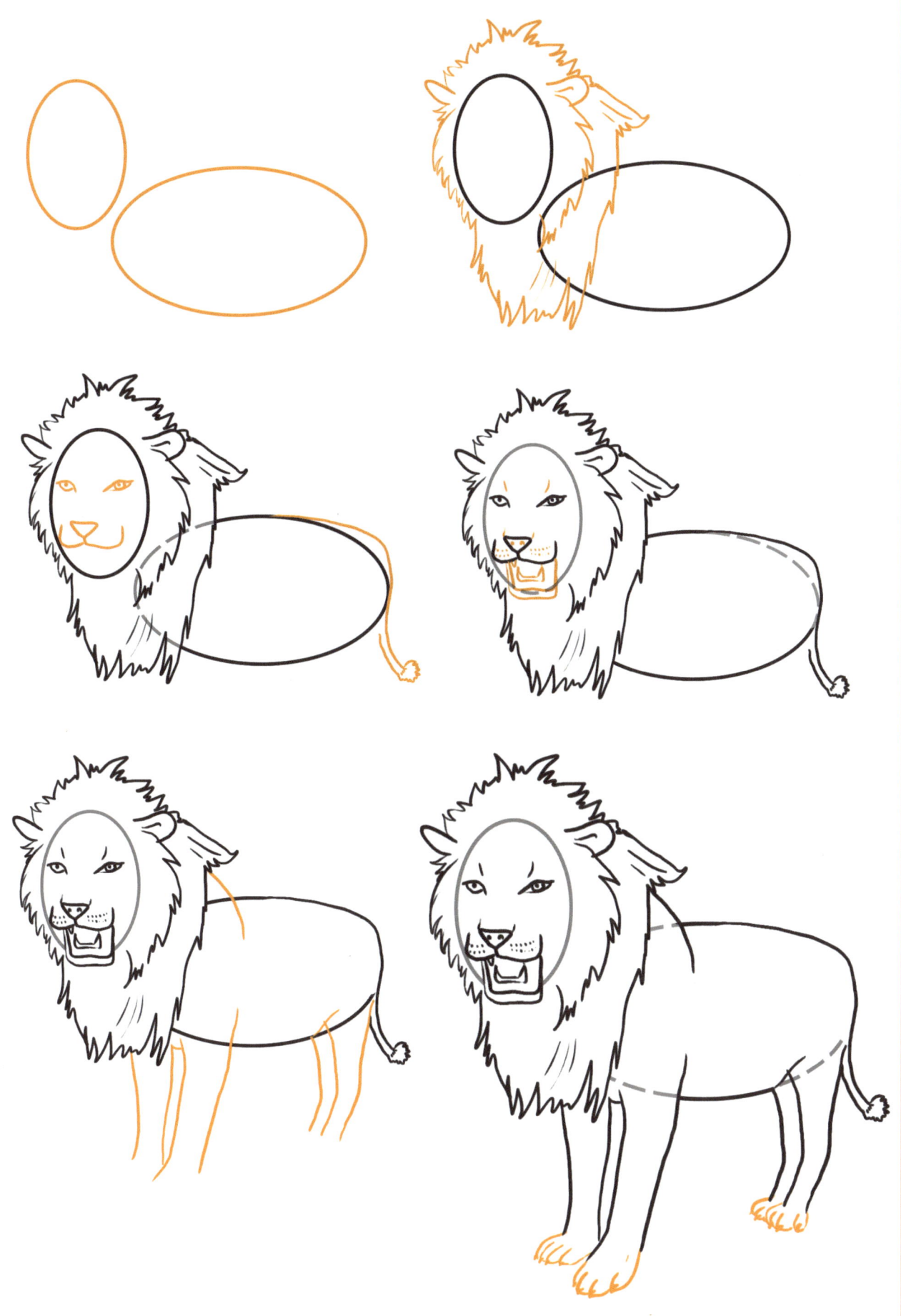

I Heard You Can Draw a...
Turkey!

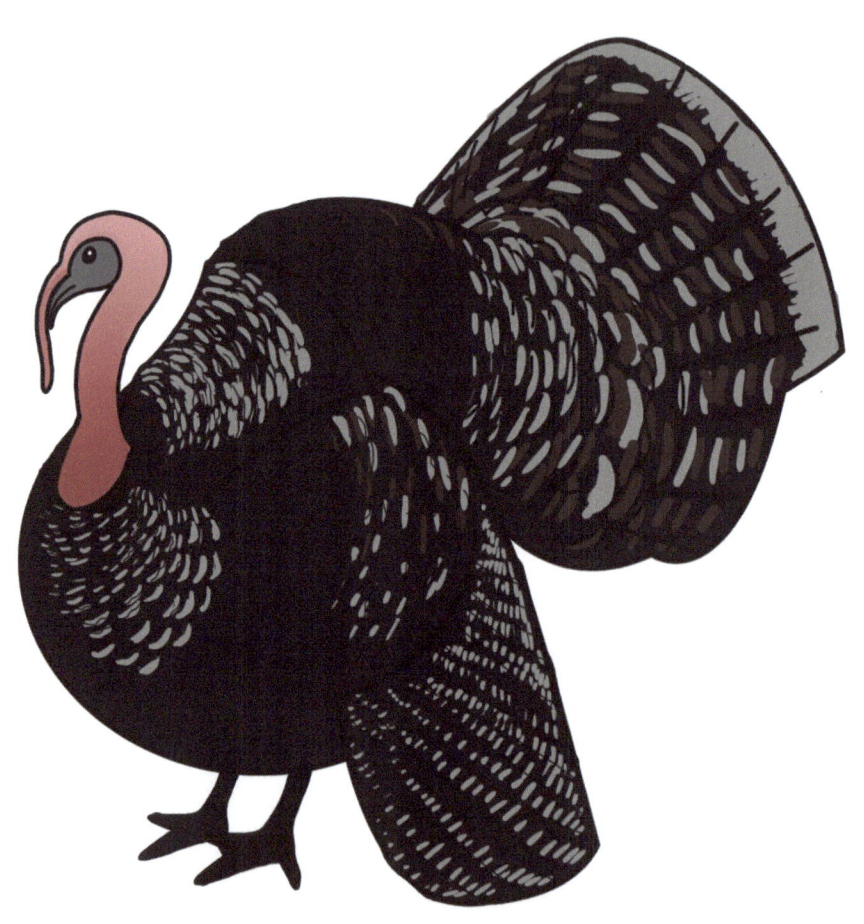

Turkeys are native to North America. Male turkeys have a red flap on their beaks called a snood.

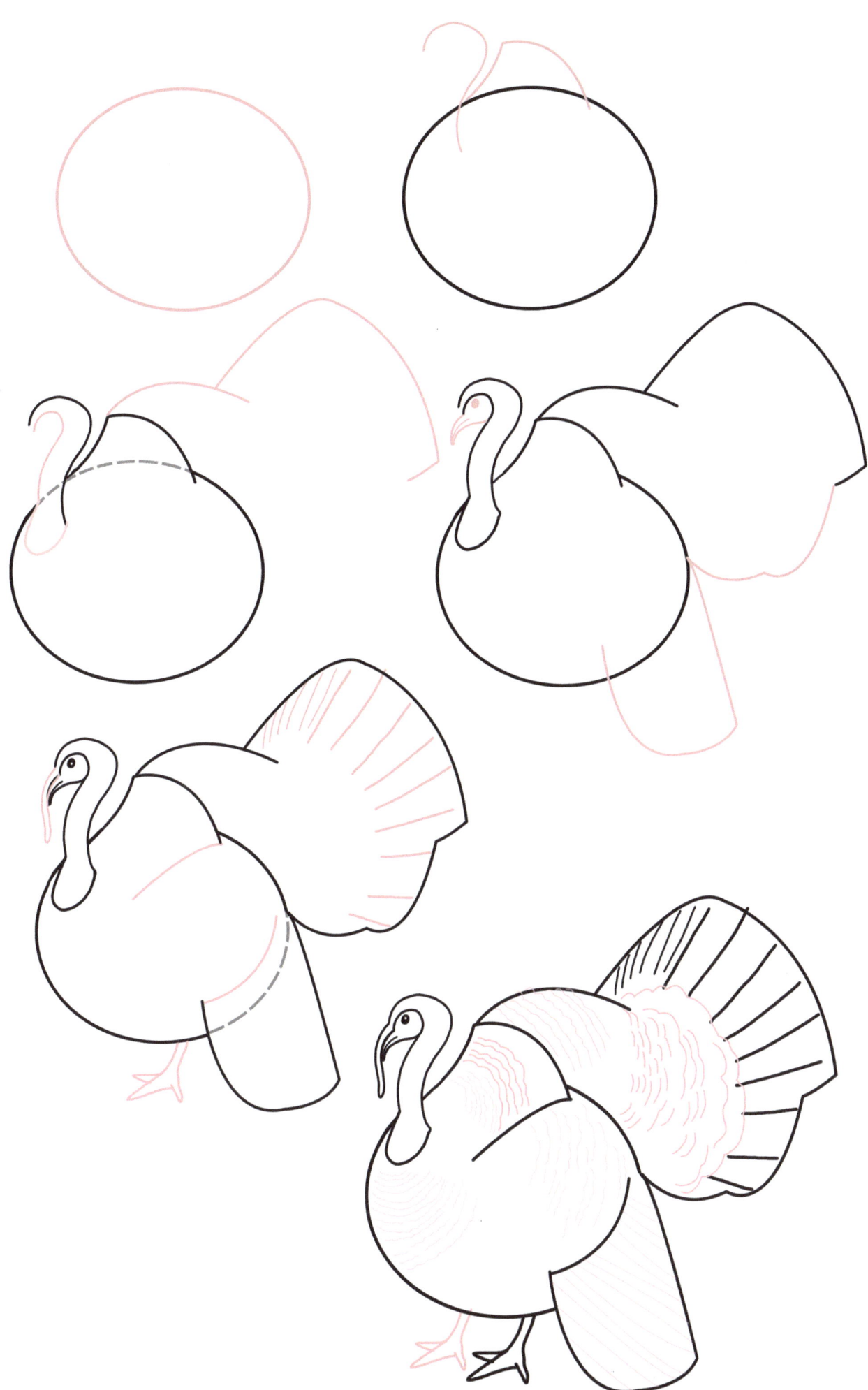

I Heard You Can Draw a...
Rabbit!

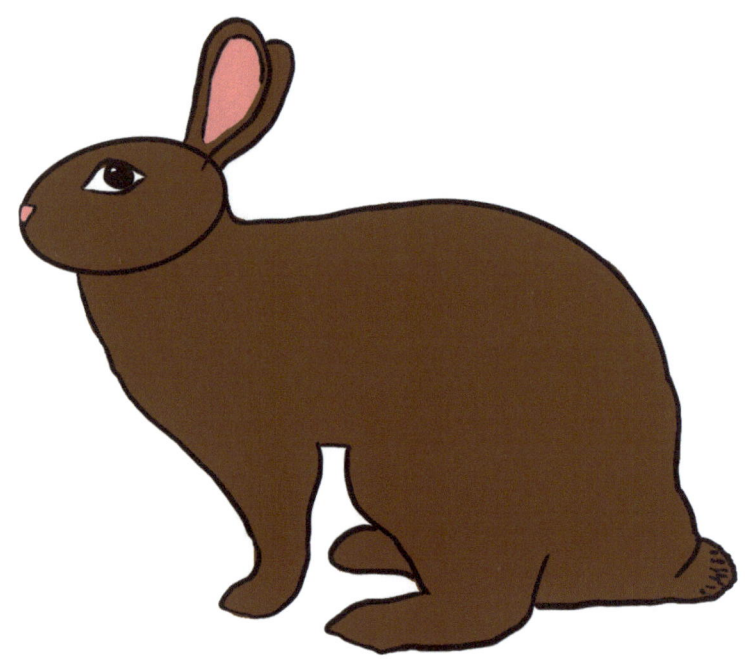

Rabbits are mammals that live mostly in North America.
They are herbivores which means that they only eat plants.

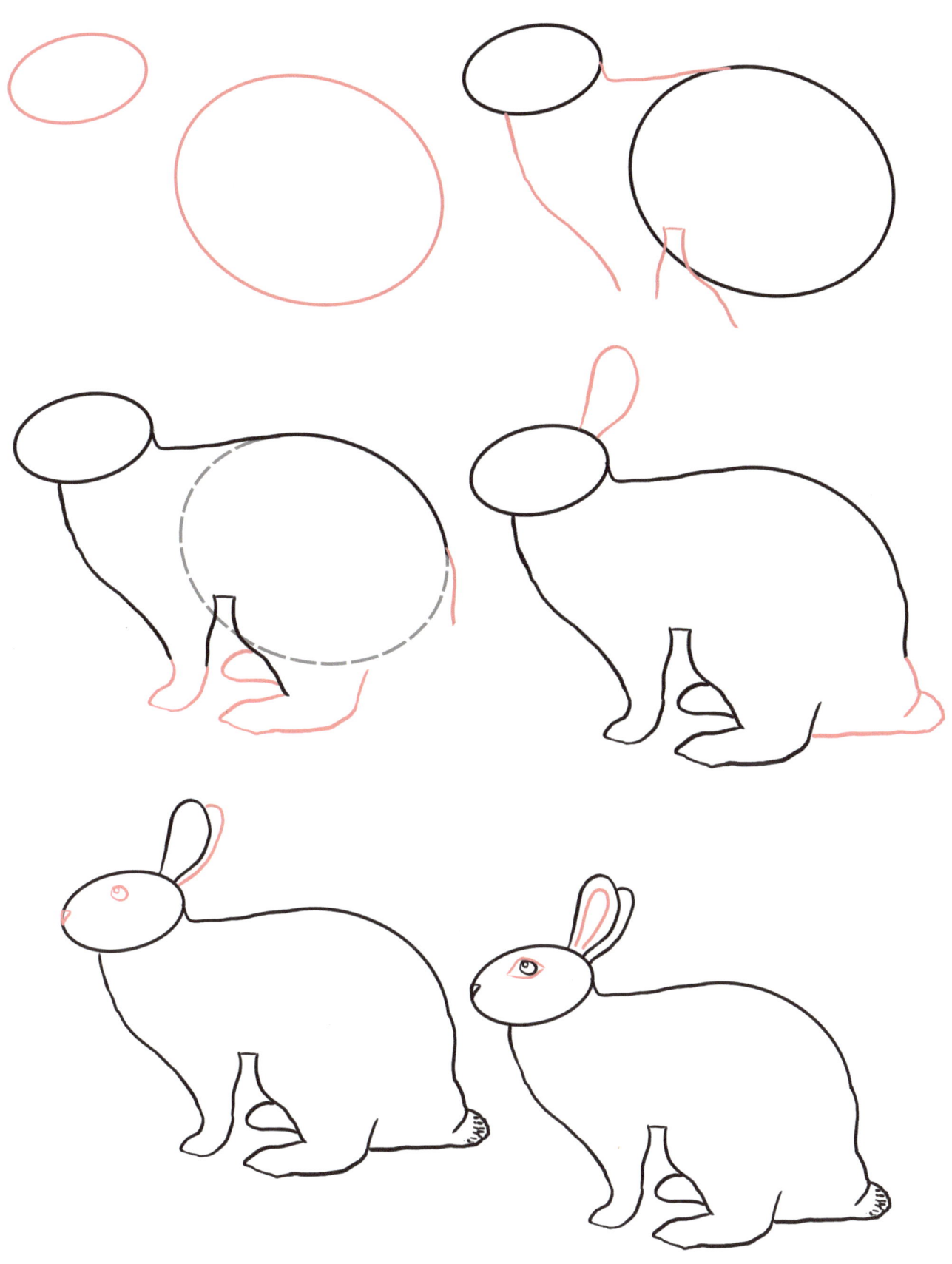

I Heard You Can Draw a...
Barbary Sheep!

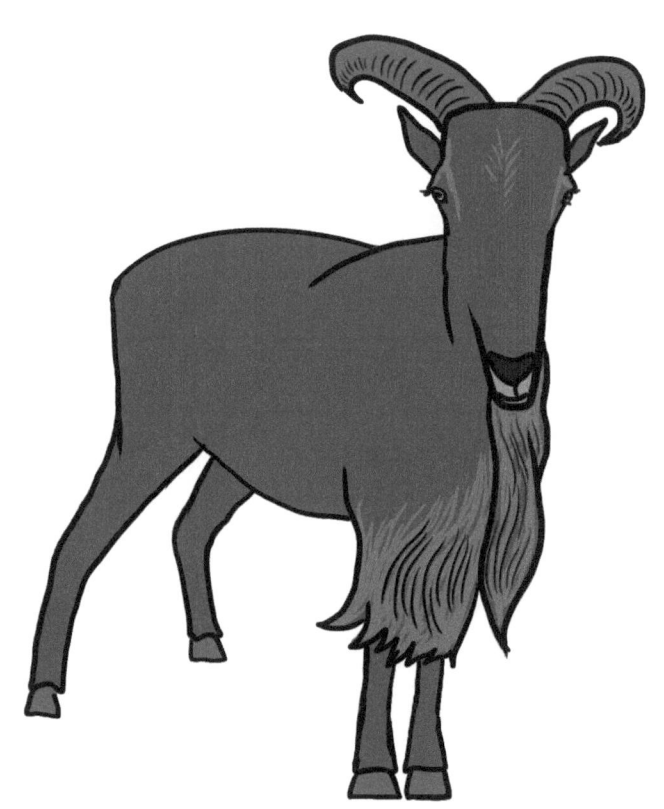

Barbary Sheep have large, curved horns.
They have long hair under the chin and on the chest.
They live in North Africa where they are also known as Aoudads.

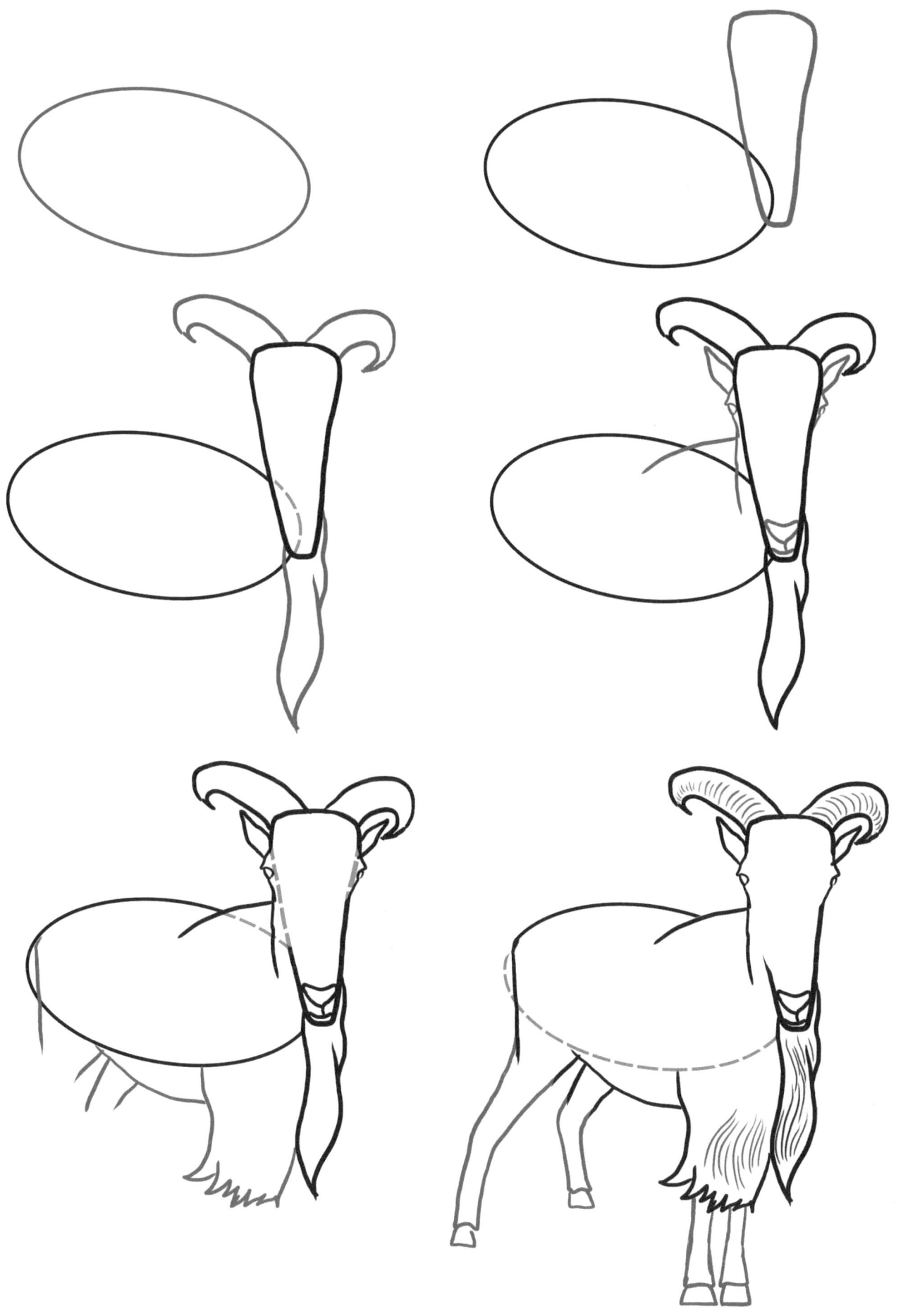

I Heard You Can Draw a...
Patagonian Cavy!

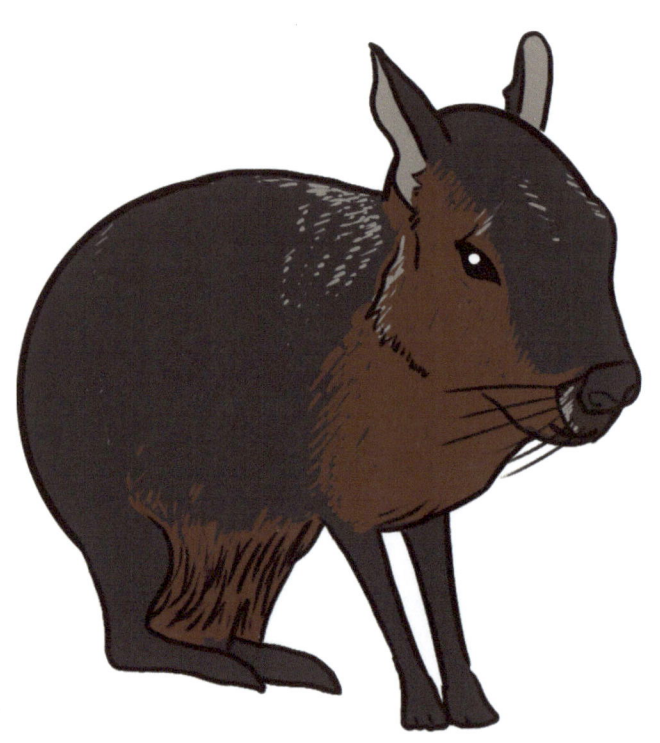

The Patagonian Cavy lives in Argentina. They are rodents and are also known as Patagonian Maras.

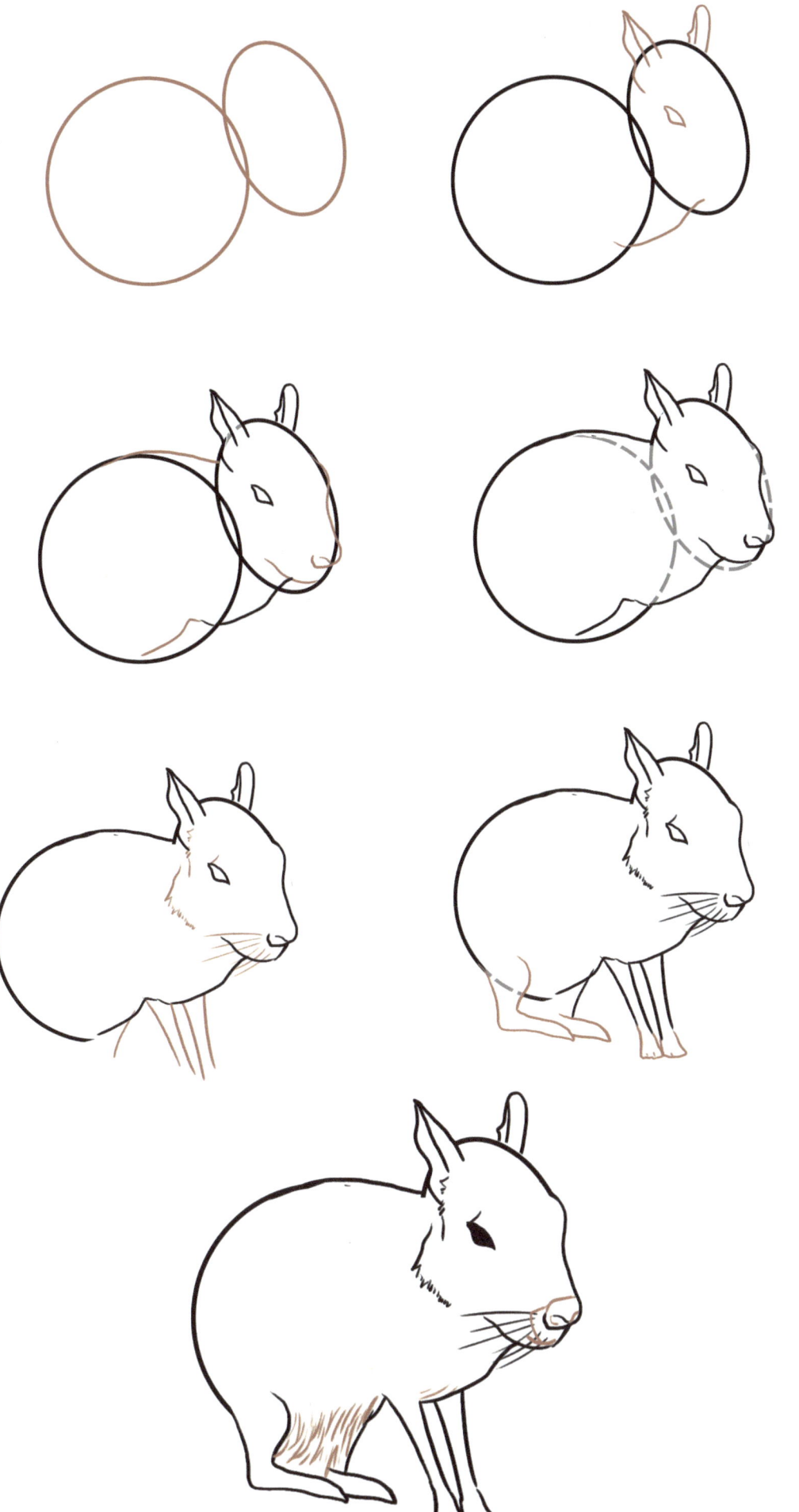

I Heard You Can Draw an...
Elephant!

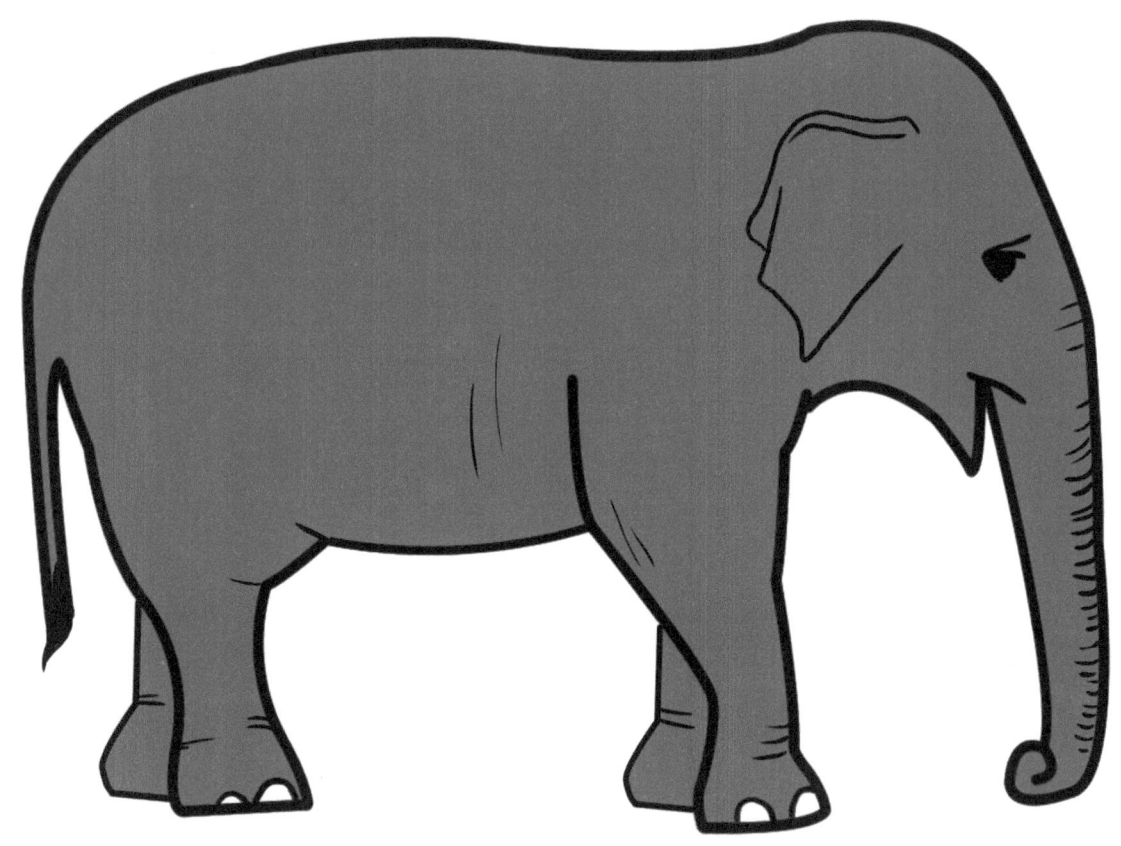

Asian elephants are smaller than African elephants.
Female Asian elephants do not have tusks like the males.
They are herbivores and they can use their trunks to grab objects.

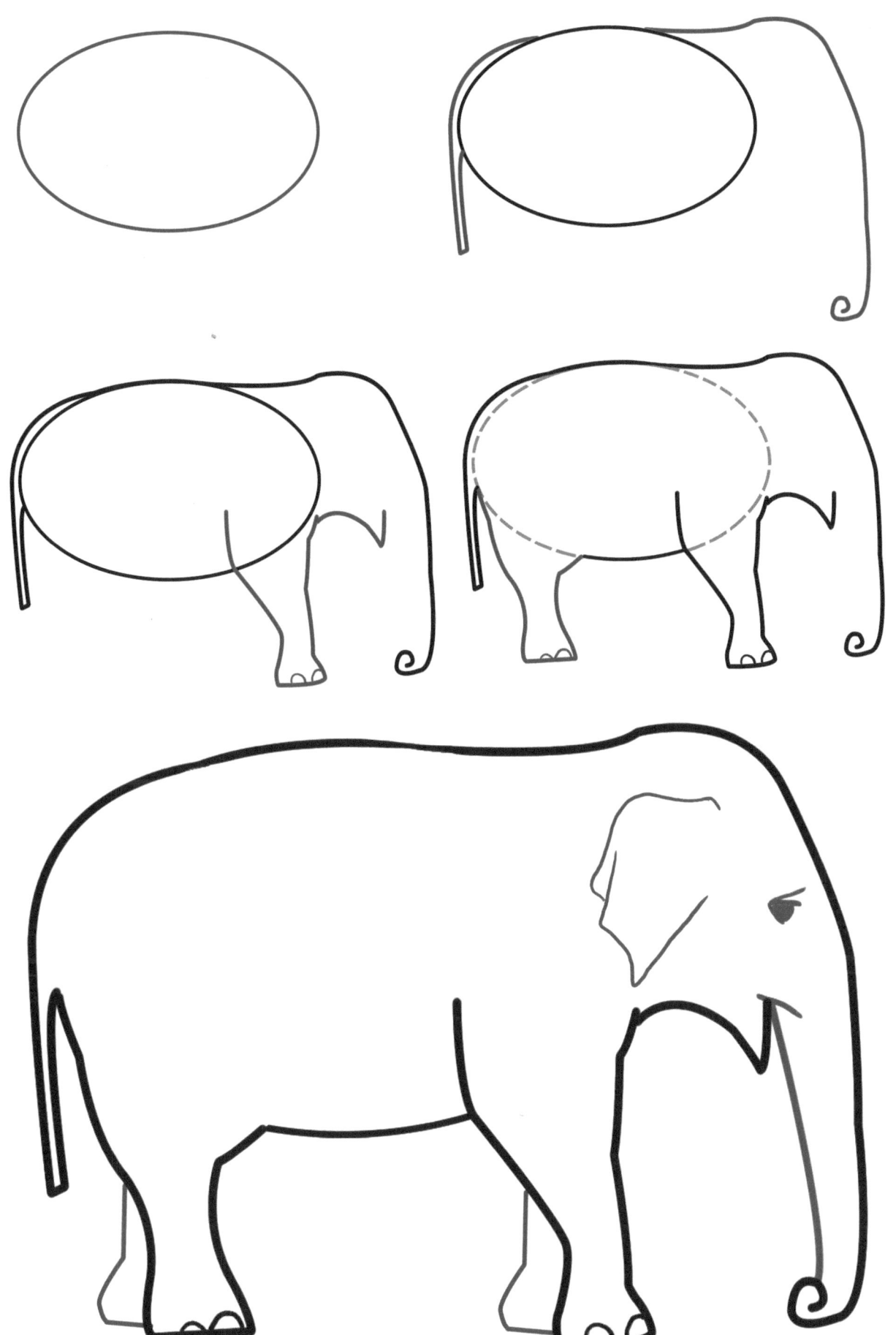

I Heard You Can Draw a...
Rhinoceros!

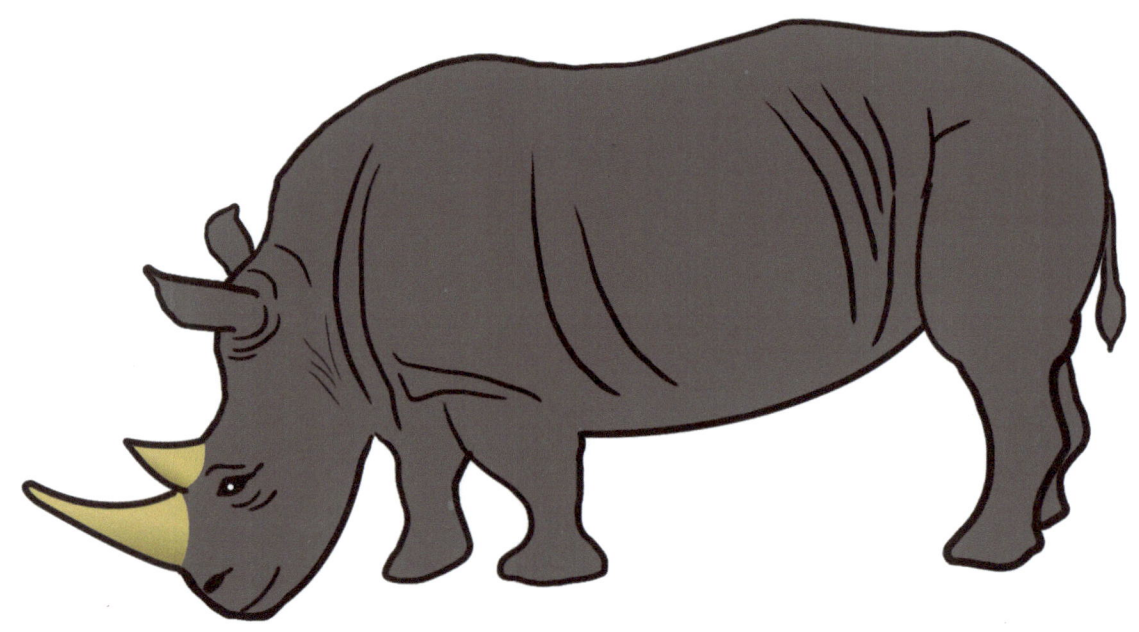

Rhinoceroses are herbivores, so they only eat plants.
They weigh thousands of pounds and have very thick skin!
They live in Africa and Asia and they are considered
to be endangered.

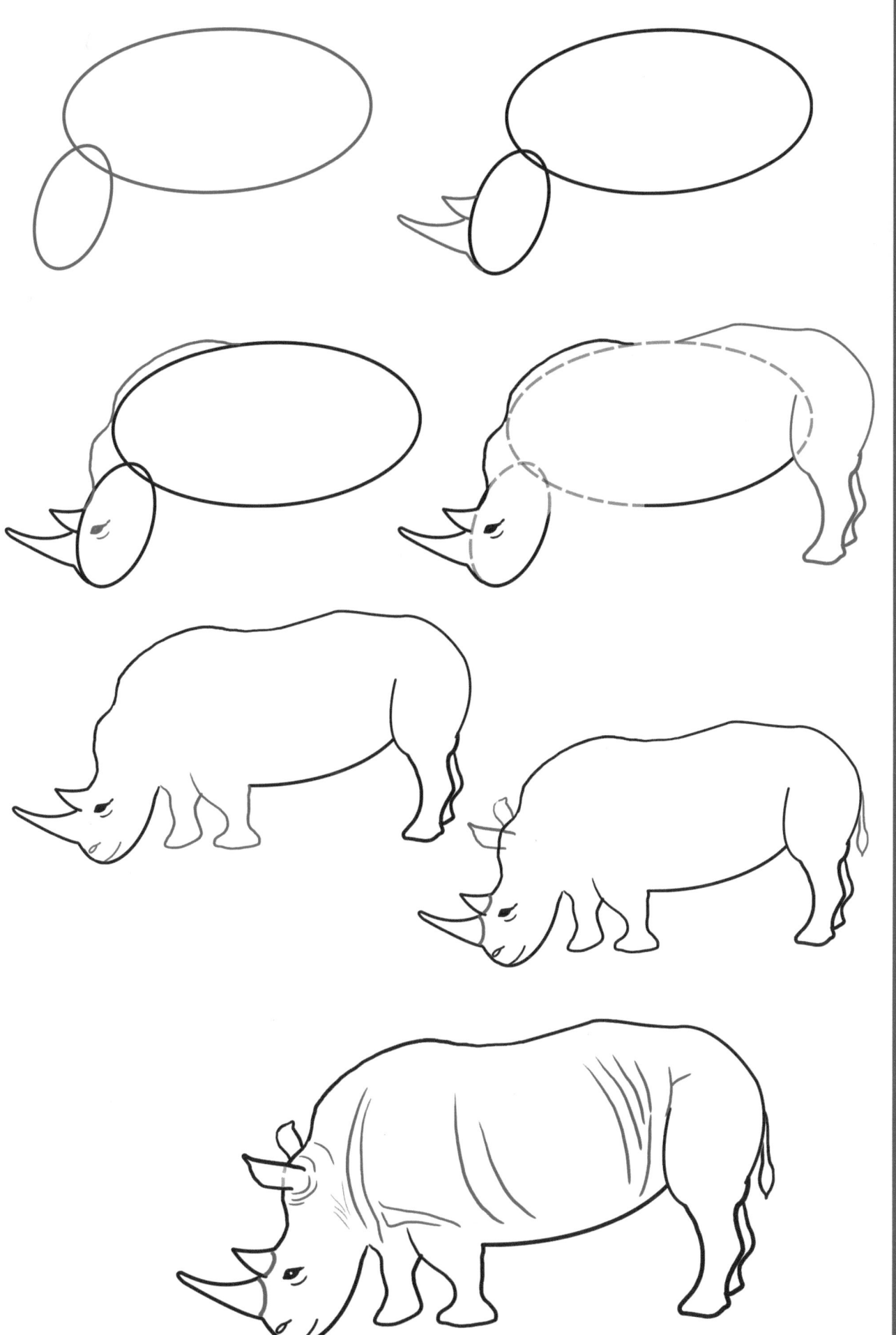

33

I Heard You Can Draw an...
African Penguin!

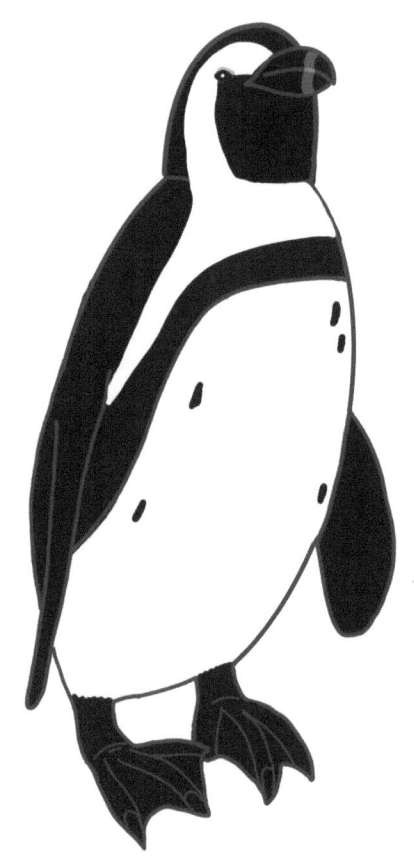

African penguins have black and white bodies.
They like to swim and eat fish!

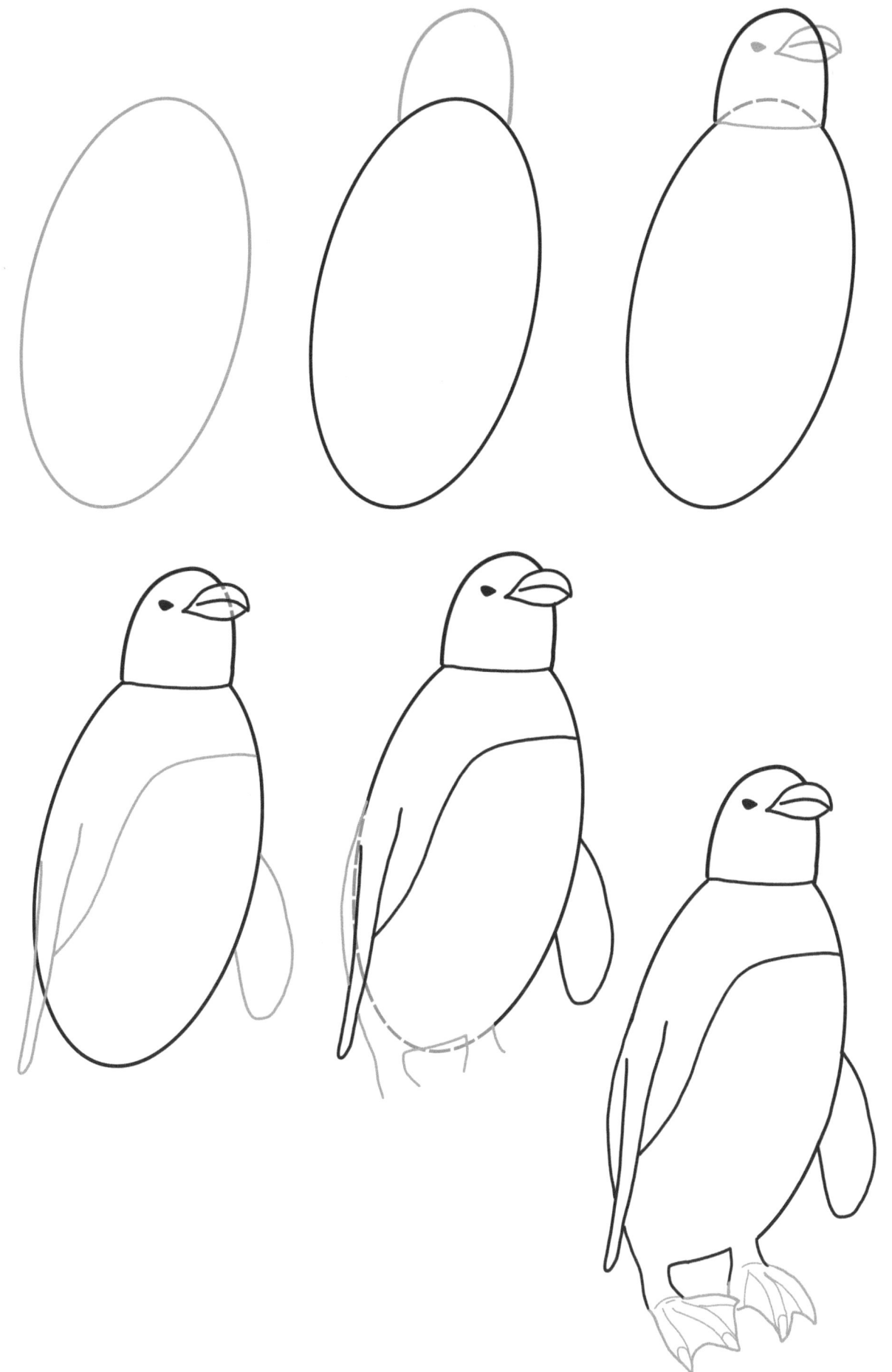

I Heard You Can Draw an...
Aardvark!

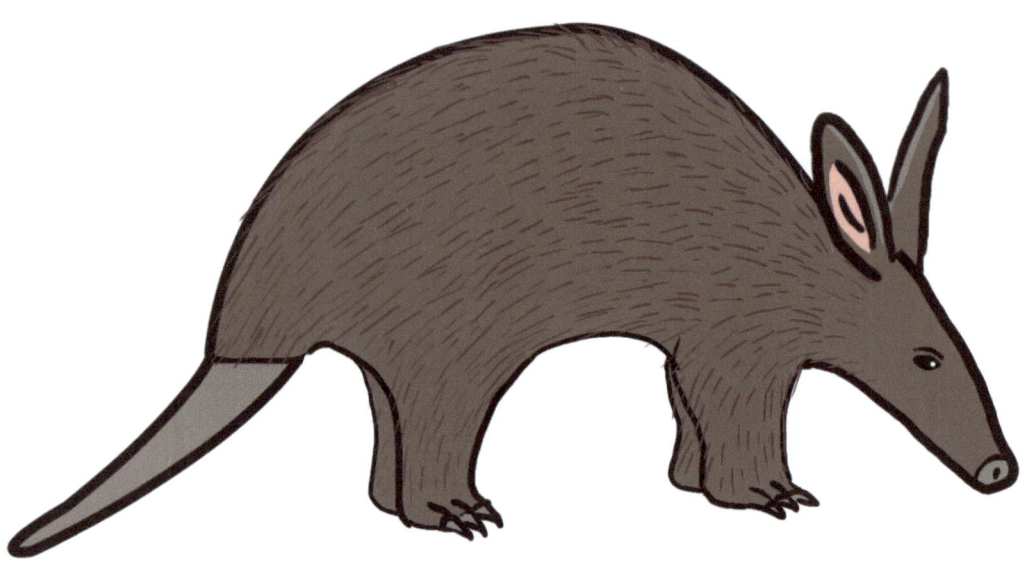

Aardvarks live in Africa. They are nocturnal which means that they sleep during the day and are active at night.
They are very good at digging holes with their strong claws.
Aardvarks mostly eat termites.

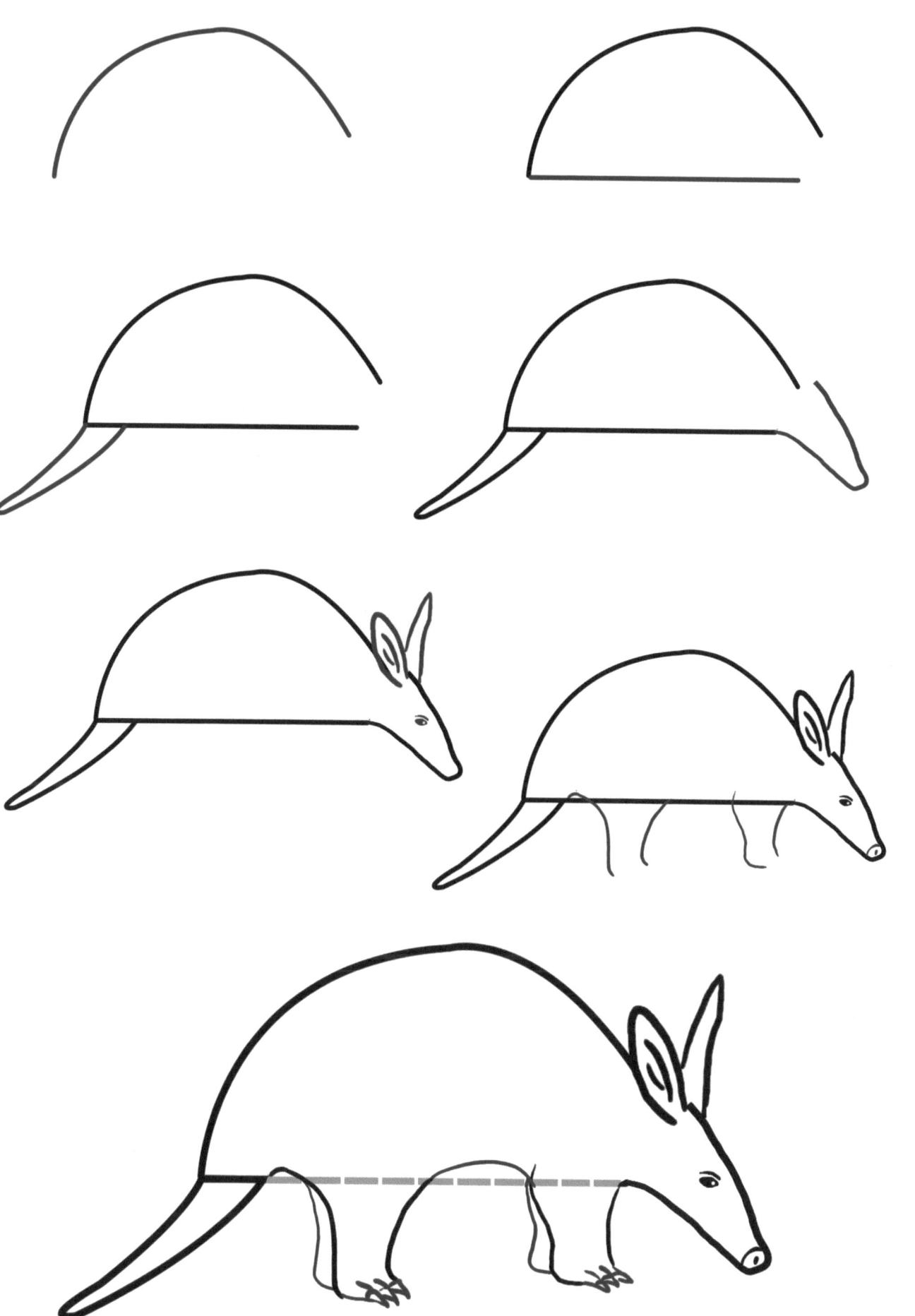

I Heard You Can Draw a...
Rattlesnake!

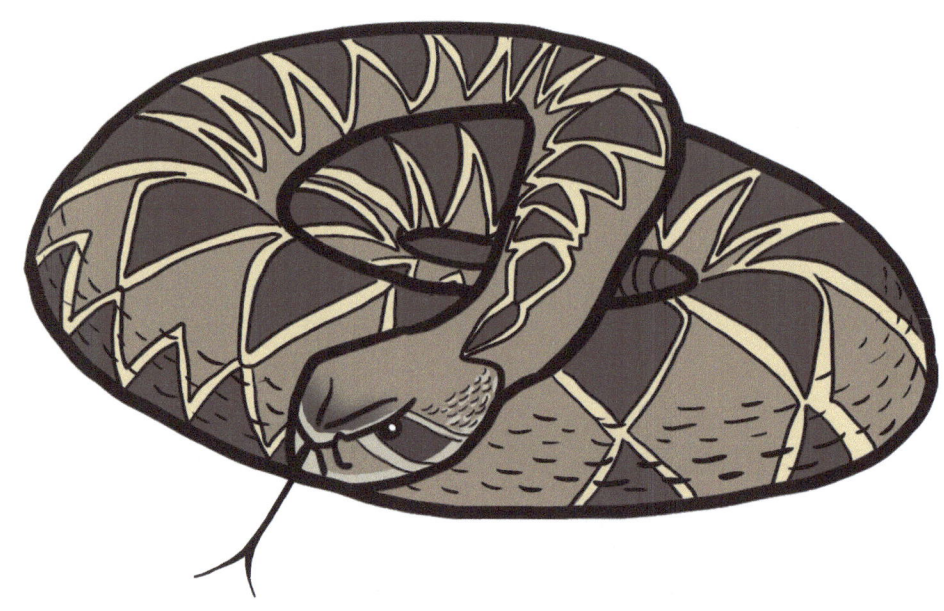

Rattlesnakes shake their noisy tails to scare away potential predators!
They eat small animals, like mice and rats, using their venomous teeth.

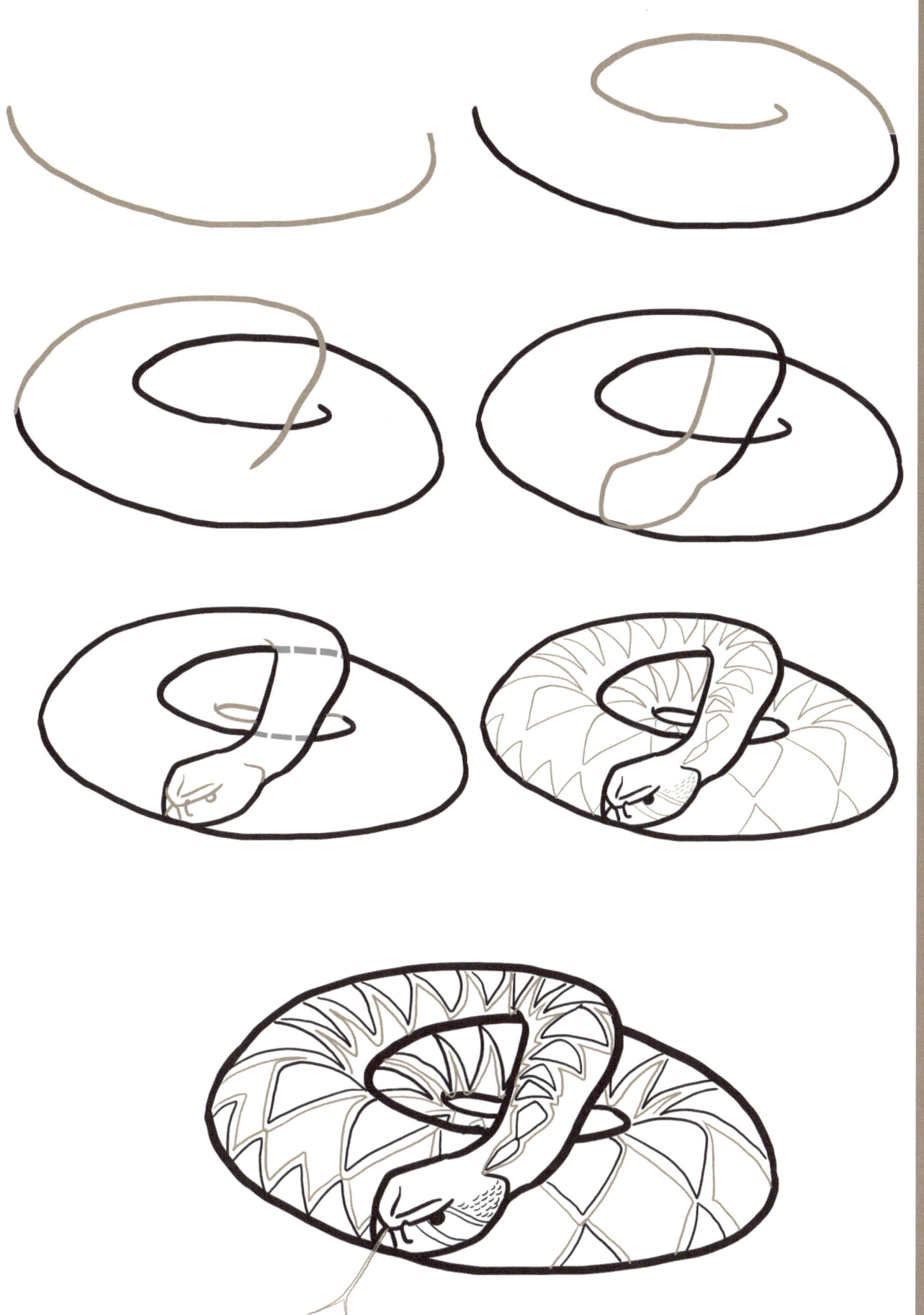

I Heard You Can Draw an...
Alligator!

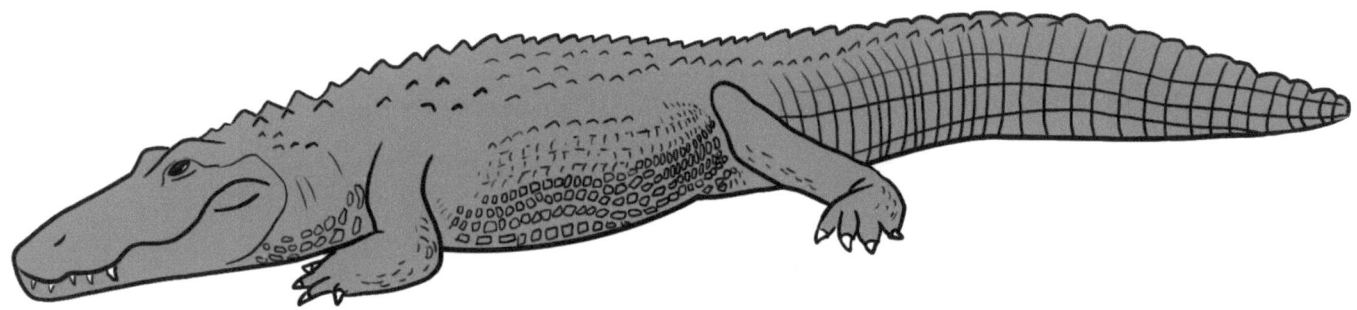

American Alligators are very large reptiles.
They can grow to be fifteen feet long! They have very
strong tails that help them swim fast.

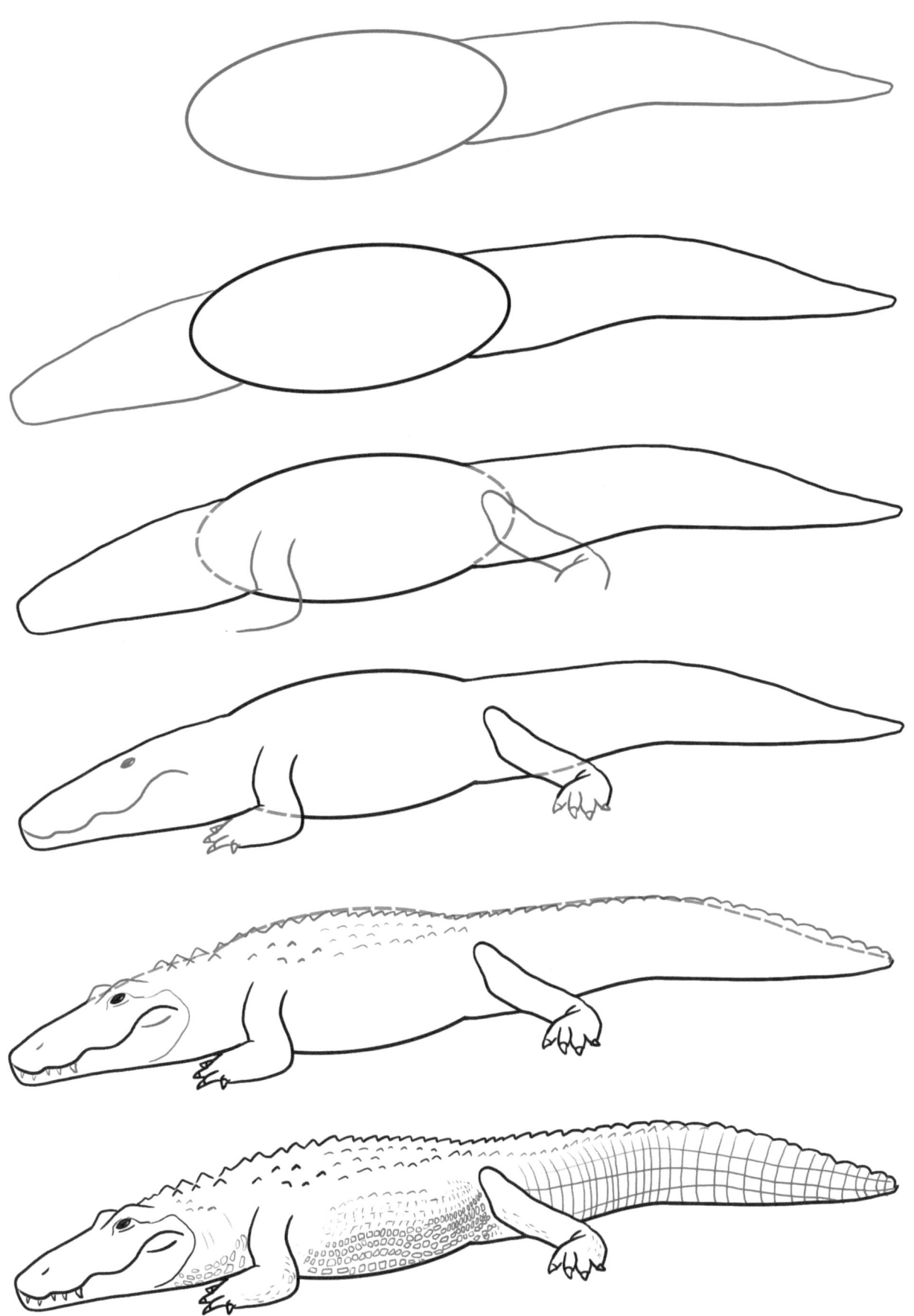

Index

Collect them all!

Visit: IHeardYouCanDraw.tumblr.com

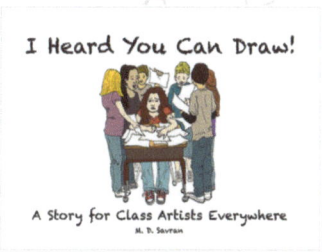

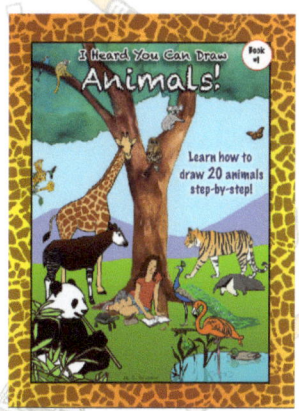 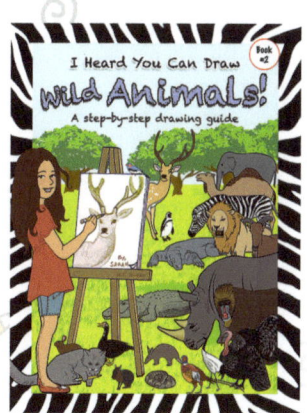

I Heard You Can Draw!
A Story for Class Artists Everywhere
40p Paperback
A picture book about a girl who loves to draw. She discovers how to follow her heart after classmates find out that she has this special talent.

I Heard You Can Draw Animals! (Book #1)
I Heard You Can Draw Wild Animals! (Book #2)

Artist Sketchbooks

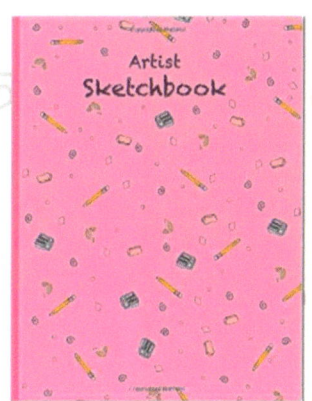 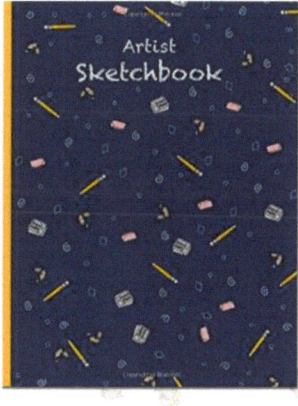 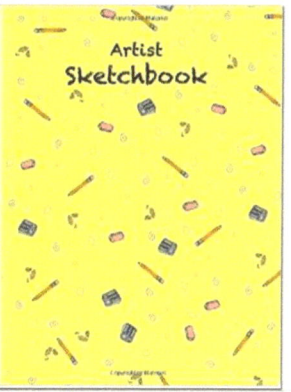 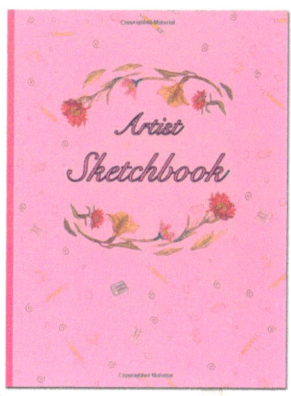

Pink / Navy / Yellow / Pink Flower
60 blank pages

Art Class with Ms. S. Books